the

BULLS

by Roland Lazenby

a Pocket Primer

BULLS 33

BULLS 25

BULLS

BULLS 9

BULLS 13

ADDAX
PUBLISHING
GROUP

Published by Addax Publishing Group
Copyright © 1998 by Roland Lazenby
Designed by Randy Breeden
Cover Design by Jerry Hirt

Library of Congress Cataloging-in-Publication Data

Lazenby, Roland.
    The unofficial Chicago Bulls pocket primer / by Roland
Lazenby.
        p. cm.
    ISBN 1-886110-41-7
    1. Chicago Bulls (Basketball team)—History. I. Title.
    GV885.52.C45L398   1998
    796.323'64'0977311—dc21   98-17576
                                                    CIP

Distributed to the trade by Andrews McMeel
4520 Main Street
Kansas City, MO 64111

Printed in the United States of America
1 3 5 7 9 10 8 6 4 2

CONTENTS

3

What is your favorite moment in Chicago Bulls championship history?

For longtime assistant coach Tex Winter, that moment was the team's first NBA championship in 1991.

For Michael Jordan, it was the fourth title, in 1996. "That's the first time I really came back and focused on my career without my father," he said. "That was probably my best."

Every Bulls fan has a host of special memories, and now you can trace hundreds of them in this handy guide to Chicago's glory years. You can join the team in 1984 with Jordan and follow step by step as he, Phil Jackson, Jerry Krause, Scottie Pippen and a host of teammates build a grand championship tradition.

It's a simple format. Flip through the pages, find your favorite moment and dig into the excitement.

Michael Jordan left the University of North Carolina after his junior season in 1984 and entered the NBA draft. The Houston Rockets selected center Hakeem Olajuwon first. With the second pick, the Portland Trail Blazers took Kentucky center Sam Bowie, leaving many observers dumfounded. Waiting with the third pick were the Chicago Bulls, who grabbed Jordan.

Portland's mistake would go down as the greatest blunder in draft history.

Jordan led the U.S. to the Olympic gold medal in Los Angeles that summer, then exploded into an instant phenomenon that fall when he joined the NBA.

Bill Blair, who was then a Bulls' assistant coach, recalled that head coach Kevin Loughery decided to have a scrimmage on the second day of practice to see if Jordan was going to be as good as the team thought. "Michael took the ball off the rim at one end," Blair said, "and went to the other end. From the top of the key, he soared in and dunked it, and Kevin says, 'We don't have to scrimmage anymore.'"

"When we started doing one-on-one drills," Loughery recalled, "we immediately saw that we had a star. I can't say that we knew we had the best player ever in basketball. But we always felt that Michael could shoot the ball. A lot of people had questioned that. But Michael had played in a passing game system in college under Dean Smith and in the Olympics under Bobby Knight. So people never got the opportunity to see him handle the ball individually the way he could handle it.

"We saw his skills, but you've got to be around him every day to see the competitiveness of the guy. He was gonna try to take over every situation that was difficult. He was gonna put himself on the line. He enjoyed it. But as much as you talk about Michael's offensive ability, he's probably one of the best

◀ Early Air Jordan.

defensive players to play the game. His anticipation was so great, he could see the floor, his quickness, and then his strength. That's another thing that's overlooked, how strong Michael is. He really had the whole package."

EARLY RETURNS

"You knew you had somebody special because Michael was always there at practice 45 minutes early," Bill Blair recalled. "He wanted to work on his shooting. And after practice he'd make you help him. He'd keep working on his shooting. He didn't care how long he was out there. The thing that I always loved about him, when you'd take him out in practice to give him a rest during a scrimmage, he was constantly back on you to get him back in. Michael loved to play the game."

Jordan scored 27 points in an early loss to the Celtics in Chicago Stadium. "I've never seen one player turn a team around like that," Larry Bird, the league's reigning Most Valuable Player, said afterward. "All the Bulls have become better because of him. . . Pretty soon this place will be packed every night. . . They'll pay just to watch Jordan. He's the best. Even at this stage in his career, he's doing more than I ever did. I couldn't do what he does as a rookie. Heck, there was one drive tonight. He had the ball up in his right hand, then he took it down. Then he brought it back up. I got a hand on it, fouled him, and he still scored. All the while, he's in the air.

"You have to play this game to know how difficult that is. You see that and say, 'Well, what the heck can you do?'

"I'd seen a little of him before and wasn't that impressed. I mean, I thought he'd be good, but not this good. Ain't nothing he can't do. That's good for this franchise, good for the league."

In just his ninth pro game, Jordan scored 45 points against San Antonio. Six weeks later he burned Cleveland for another 45. Then came a 42-point performance against New York. Another 45 against Atlanta, and his first triple-double (35 points, 15 assists and 14 rebounds) against Denver. Then, just before the All-Star break, he zipped in 41 against defending champion Boston.

It wasn't just Jordan's point totals that thrilled the crowds. His appeal began with his energy level. He played all-out, every minute. On defense, he was a roaming thief. On offense, he was simply a cornucopia. Jumpers. Elegant dunks. Reverses. Finger rolls. Short bank shots. All executed with a style that bordered on miraculous. When he couldn't get to the hoop by land, he traveled by air. Literally, he could fly. (The definition of flying, according to the Random House Dictionary of the English Language, is "to be carried through the air by the wind or any other force or agency.")

For the first time in their history, the "force" was with the Bulls, and it meant a profound transformation for both the team and its young superstar. Chicago had joined the NBA in 1966 as an expansion franchise and had suffered through two decades of frustration. The Bulls had fallen into deep misery in the half-dozen seasons before Jordan's arrival, and crowds in Chicago Stadium had dwindled to a few thousand many nights.

The fans returned in droves to see Jordan, although he still didn't generate regular sellouts that first season. The Bulls would have to become winners to draw regular crowds.

Seeing that the Bulls' young star was going places, Nike soon built a multimillion-dollar shoe and clothing deal around his image. Michael, the player, quickly became Air Jordan, the incredibly successful corporate entity. Before long, he was making far more money off the court than on it. Rather than dull his unique drive, this off-court success seemed to shove it into a higher gear.

"He's as much an image as he is a symbol," agent David Falk had said late that October 1984 after revealing that Jordan had already signed promotional deals with Nike, Wilson Sporting Goods and the Chicagoland Chevrolet Dealerships Association. The Nike deal alone paid him $500,000 per year. "I know everybody's eyes are on me," Jordan said, "and some of the things I do even surprise myself. They aren't always planned. They just happen."

Jordan's second coach was Stan Albeck, seen here cheering on
Gene Banks' hustle.

ENTER THE TWO JERRYS

To build around Jordan, new Bulls chairman Jerry Reinsdorf, who had taken control of the team in 1985, brought in longtime scout Jerry Krause to run the basketball operations. They soon became known around Chicago as "the two Jerrys," because they worked so closely together, almost like Siamese twins.

After two decades of upheaval and misfires in the team's front office, Bulls fans were openly leery of Krause's seemingly unorthodox approach. There were early missteps greeted by loud hisses from the media and fans. In retrospect, it seems obvious that a pattern of success was emerging. But at the time, the entire enterprise was a burgeoning gamble with careers on the line. The primary casualties were coaches. First, coach Kevin Loughery was fired and replaced by Stan Albeck. After one season, Krause and Reinsdorf fired Albeck and hired Doug Collins, a former pro player and TV analyst who had never coached.

Jordan had led the lowly Bulls to the playoffs that first year, where they quickly lost to Milwaukee. The next season, 1986, with Stan Albeck at the helm, Jordan overcame a serious foot injury to carry them into the playoffs once more, where they were vanquished 3-0 by Boston, but not before Jordan scared the Celtics blue by scoring 63 points in one game, an NBA playoffs record.

Then Collins took over, and Jordan went on from there, shoving the Bulls a notch higher each year. And in the process, he claimed nearly every major individual achievement imaginable. By the 1991 playoffs, he had captured the league scoring title five times. He had been named the league's Most Valuable Player twice. He had been named to the All-NBA first team five times in seven years.

But, alas, the Bulls had won nothing. In 1987, the Celtics again swept them in the first round of the playoffs. In 1988, they beat Cleveland, then fell to the Detroit Pistons in the Eastern semifinals. In 1989, they advanced to the conference finals with wins over Cleveland and New York, but again ran into the Pistons and lost, 4-2.

Phil Jackson moved in as head coach after the firing of Doug Collins.

FIRING COLLINS, PROMOTING JACKSON

Krause responded to the 1989 playoff loss by firing the popular Collins and promoting assistant Phil Jackson, a former NBA player and Continental Basketball Association coach who hadn't been able to find a coaching job in the NBA until Krause hired him. All kinds of rumors swirled around Chicago after Collins' firing. After all, the Bulls had just enjoyed one of the most successful seasons in team history.

Bulls' management insisted Collins was released because his coaching style was too frenetic for his players.

Jackson's first move was to adopt the triple-post offensive scheme of veteran Bulls assistant Tex Winter. Winter had been the first person Krause had hired upon being named GM in 1985, and Krause wanted the team to use Winter's offensive ideas. But Stan Albeck and Doug Collins had largely ignored Winter's advice.

Jackson, however, had won a championship ring as a member of the 1973 New York Knicks, and he had decided to have an offense that featured the ball movement of Winter's system and a defense that offered opponents nothing but pressure.

"When Phil came in, our first training camp was as difficult a camp as I'd ever had," recalled former Bulls guard John Paxson. "It was defensive-oriented. Everything we did was, start from the defensive end and work to the offensive end. Phil basically made us into a pressure-type team. Defensively, he knew that was how we would win."

"We were gonna play full-court pressure defense," Jackson said. "We were gonna throw our hearts into it."

Jerry Krause snared Horace Grant and Scottie Pippen in the 1987 draft.

THE DOBERMANS

A huge factor in the Bulls' success was the drafting of Scottie Pippen and Horace Grant in 1987. Once the two rookies were secured for Chicago, people across the organization began to sense that the Bulls were about to undergo dramatic change.

It took a few seasons for them to mature, but Pippen and Grant would become major weapons in the pressure defense Jackson planned to deploy. The two young players possessed enough athleticism to give the defense its bite. Assistant coach Johnny Bach called them the Dobermans. "He's on the cusp of greatness," Bach said of Pippen in 1990. "He's starting to do the kinds of things only Michael does."

"It's just a matter of working hard," Pippen said at the time. "I've worked to improve my defense and shooting off the dribble. I know I'm a better spot-up shooter, but I'm trying to pull up off the dribble when the lane is blocked."

Jordan led the Bulls in scoring, but it was Pippen who gave opposing coaches nightmares. Few teams had a means of matching up with him, particularly when they also had to worry about Jordan.

The Pistons seemed to overpower Jordan and his teammates in the early days.

SPANKED BY THE
BULLIES AGAIN

A series of win streaks propelled the Bulls to a 55–27 finish in 1990, good for second place in the Central division behind the 60-win Pistons, the defending World Champions. And Jordan harvested another batch of honors: All-NBA, All-Defense, and his fourth consecutive scoring title. Plus he led the league in steals.

The Bulls sailed into the playoffs with new confidence and Pippen playing like a veteran. First they dismissed the Milwaukee Bucks and followed that by humbling Charles

15

Barkley and the Philadelphia 76ers. But Pippen's 70-year-old father, Lewis, died during the series, and the young forward rushed home to Arkansas for the funeral. He returned in time to help finish off Philly. Next up were the Pistons and the Eastern Finals. In essence, it was the big exam for Jackson's new style of play. The series was a gauntlet. The year before in the playoffs, Bill Laimbeer had knocked Pippen out of Game 6 with an elbow to the head. The Detroit center claimed the shot was inadvertent, but that wasn't the way the Bulls saw it. To win a championship this time around, the Chicago coaches and players knew they had to stand up to the "Bad Boys."

"I thought they were thugs," Jerry Reinsdorf said of the Pistons, "and you know, you have to hold the ownership responsible for that. I mean, Billy Laimbeer was a thug. He would hit people from behind in the head during dead balls. He took cheap shots all the time. Mahorn and lunatic Rodman, I mean, they tried to hurt people."

"There were times," Pippen said, "a few years before the fla-grant foul rules, when guys would have a breakaway and [the Pistons] would cut their legs out from under them. Anything to win a game. That's not the way the game is supposed to be played. I remember once when Michael had a breakaway, and Laimbeer took him out. There was no way he could have blocked the shot. When you were out there playing them, that was always in the back of your mind, to kind of watch yourself."

HEADACHES

The Bulls thought they were ready to challenge Detroit in 1990. At first, their conference final series seemed to develop as a classic, with each team winning tight battles at home to tie it at 3-3 heading into Game 7 at the Palace of Auburn Hills. The Pistons had homecourt advantage, yet the Bulls had worked for years to get to this point. But things went dreadfully wrong, beginning with Paxson limping from a badly sprained ankle and Pippen developing a migraine headache just before tipoff.

"Scottie had had migraines before," Bulls trainer Mark Pfeil explained. "He actually came to me before the game and said he couldn't see. I said, 'Can you play?' He started to tell me no, and Michael jumped in and said, 'Hell, yes, he can play. Start him. Let him play blind.'

"Horace Grant kind of backed up a little bit that game, too,"

Pfeil added. "It was more a matter of maturity than wimpin' out. It took a certain period of time before they would stand up and say, 'Damn it, I've been pushed to the wall enough.' Scottie played with the headache, and as the game went on he got better."

Pippen played, but the entire roster seemed lost. The Bulls fell into a deep hole in the second quarter and never climbed out. With the Bad Boys flying their skull 'n' crossbones banners and their 'Bad to the Bone' theme music playing, the Pistons advanced easily, 93-74.

"My worst moment as a Bull was trying to finish out the seventh game that we lost to the Pistons in the Palace," Jackson recalled. "There was Scottie Pippen with a migraine on the bench, and John Paxson had sprained his ankle in the game before. I just had to sit there and grit my teeth and go through a half in which we were struggling to get in the ballgame. We had just gone through a second period that was an embarrassment to the organization. It was my most difficult moment as a coach."

Furious with his teammates, Jordan cursed them at halftime, then sobbed in the back of the team bus afterward. "I was crying and steaming," he recalled. "I was saying, 'Hey, I'm out here busting my butt and nobody else is doing the same thing. These guys are kicking our butt, taking our heart, taking our pride.' I made up my mind right then and there it would never happen again. That was the summer that I first started lifting weights. If I was going to take some of this beating, I was also going to start dishing out some of it. I got tired of them dominating me physically."

CHARACTER QUESTIONS

With each Chicago loss in the playoffs, observers grew more convinced that the Bulls were flawed because Jordan made them virtually a one-man team. Some pointed out that it had taken Wilt Chamberlain, Jerry West and Oscar Robertson many years to lead teams to the NBA title. Some critics said Jordan fit into the category with those players. Others wondered if he wasn't headed for the same anguish as Elgin Baylor, Nate Thurmond, Pete Maravich and Dave Bing, all great players who never played on a championship team.

Jordan was understandably angered by such speculation and by the criticism that he was a one-man team. In some ways, however, the burden of the loss fell on Pippen. Everyone, from the media to his own teammates, had interpreted the headache as a sign of faint-heartedness. Lost in the perspective was the fact that the third-year forward had recently buried his father.

"I'm flying back from the migraine game," recalled Chicago radio reporter Cheryl Ray, "and who should be sitting across from me but Juanita Jordan. And she says, 'What happened to Scottie?' I said, 'He had a headache.' She goes, 'He had a headache!?!?' And she just shook her head."

"It grabbed me and wouldn't let go," Pippen later said. "It's something the fans will never let die."

Bill Cartwright gave the Bulls the toughness to overcome the Pistons.

Despite the outcome, Jackson and his assistants came away from the 1990 playoffs with tremendous optimism. They knew they would have to sell Jordan and his teammates on using the triple-post offense, and they would have to get tougher defensively.

The key to their defensive toughness was 7-foot-1 Bill Cartwright, whom the Bulls had acquired from the Knicks. His career had featured one frustrating battle after another with injuries, all played out before the merciless New York media. He went through foot surgery after foot surgery, until the newspapers dubbed him "Medical Bill." The Knicks' problem was that they didn't know how to play Cartwright with Patrick Ewing. They tried putting them in a Twin Towers alignment, with modest success. Finally, they traded him to the Bulls, where Cartwright's reputation preceeded him. He had come into the league as a big-time low-post offensive threat.

But what the Bulls saw in him was the defensive intimidator they needed. Either way, Michael Jordan was not pleased to have him on the roster. Phil Jackson, however, had seen his value, not only as a defender but as a leader.

More than that, his teammates and opponents around the league knew Cartwright for his elbows. He held them high when he rebounded or boxed out. Cartwright's elbows weren't as notorious as the Pistons' style of play, but they were close. "You had to be cognizant of those elbows because they could hit you any time," recalled Bulls backup center Will Perdue. "I got hit constantly in practice. That's just the way Bill played. He was taught to play with his arms up and his elbows out."

Jordan, however, was irritated that Cartwright sometimes had trouble catching the ball, and often set up in the lane, in the way of Jordan's drives to the hoop.

"Michael really didn't know Bill Cartwright as a person," Jerry Krause said of the early troubles that developed between Jordan and Cartwright. "Michael made Bill prove himself. Michael did that with everybody. That was Michael's way. I knew what Bill was. Bill was gonna be fine with Michael. I told Bill, 'It's coming. He's gonna needle you. Michael's gonna drive you crazy.' Bill said, 'He ain't gonna do nothing to me.'"

"Michael and I had a comfort problem," Cartwright explained, "the fact that he wanted to do some things, and I was in the way. It took some getting used to. It took him getting used to me."

The relationship eased as Jordan realized that Cartwright could anchor the Bulls' defense. "One of the things that got to us," Jackson said, "was that Detroit used to have a way of bringing up the level of animosity in a game. At some level, you were gonna have to contest them physically, if you were gonna stay in the game with them. If you didn't want to stay in the game with them, fine. They'd go ahead and beat you. But if you wanted to compete, you'd have to do something physically to play at their level. Bill stood up to the Pistons. Bill's statement was, 'This isn't the way we want to play. This isn't the way I want to play. But if it is the way we have to play to take care of these guys, I'm not afraid to do it. I'm gonna show these Detroit guys this is not acceptable. We won't accept you doing this to us.' You can't imagine how much that relieved guys like Scottie Pippen and Horace Grant, guys who were being besieged constantly and challenged constantly by more physical guys like Dennis Rodman and Rick Mahorn."

FINDING THE GROOVE

With Cartwright providing the necessary toughness, Jordan and his teammates matured into a determined unit over the 1990-91 season, although their progress was sometimes frutstrating and difficult. Jordan again led the league in scoring at 31.5 points per game (to go with six rebounds and five assists per outing). A gifted swing player, Pippen performed with determination over the 1990-91 campaign, playing 3,014 minutes, averaging nearly 18 points, seven rebounds and six assists.

"I thought about it all summer," he said. "I failed to produce last season."

Pippen made the transition from being a wing into a point guard role. "He became a guy who now had the ball as much as Michael," Jackson said. He became a dominant force.

Other key factors were power forward Horace Grant (12.8 points, 8.4 rebounds); point guard John Paxson (8.7 points while jumpshooting .548 from the floor); and center Bill Cartwright (9.6 points and interior toughness on defense). Jackson also made great use of his bench with B.J. Armstrong, Craig Hodges, Will Perdue, Stacey King, Cliff Levingston, Scott Williams (a free agent rookie out of North Carolina), and

Dennis Hopson, who had come over in a trade with New Jersey, all contributing.

These efforts resulted in impressive displays of execution. In December, the Bulls' defense held the Cleveland Cavaliers to just five points in one quarter at Chicago Stadium. Crowds there presented an atmosphere that no opponent wanted to face. The Bulls lost to Boston there the third game of the season. They wouldn't lose at home again until Houston stopped them March 25, a run of 30 straight home wins.

SPANKING THE BULLIES

The Bulls won the Eastern Conference with a 61-21 record, and Jordan claimed his fifth straight scoring title with a 31.5 average. During the playoffs, he was named the league's MVP for the second time. The Bulls, however, had seen all that window dressing before. The only awards they wanted came in the playoffs. They opened against the Knicks and won the first game by a record 41 points, then went on to sweep them, 3-0. Next Charles Barkley and the 'Sixers fell, 4-1, setting up the only rematch the Bulls wanted: the Pistons in the Eastern Conference Finals.

The Bulls hammered the Pistons, who were reeling from injuries, in three straight games, and on the eve of Game 4 Jordan announced they were going to sweep. "That's not going to happen," responded an infuriated Isiah Thomas.

But it did. At the end of Game 4 the next day in Detroit, Thomas and the Pistons stalked off the floor without congratulating the Bulls, a snub that angered Jordan and thousands of Chicago fans.

"We were the white knights; we were the good guys," Jerry Reinsdorf said. "We beat the Bad Boys, 4-0, and they sulked off the court the way they did. I remember saying at the time that this was a triumph of good over evil."

Jordan celebrates the Bulls' first NBA title in 1991.

TITLE BOUT NUMBER ONE

The Portland Trail Blazers had ruled the regular season in the Western division with a 63-19 finish, but once again Magic Johnson and the Lakers survived in the playoffs, ousting Portland in the conference finals, 4-2.

For many, the Finals seemed a dream match-up: Jordan and the Bulls against Magic and the Lakers. Many observers, including former Laker coach Pat Riley, figured the Lakers' experience made them a sure bet. Los Angeles was making its ninth Finals appearance since 1980, and had five titles to show for it.

"The Lakers have experience on us," Pippen said as the series opened in Chicago Stadium, "but we have enough to win."

Just as important, the Lakers' James Worthy had a badly sprained ankle, which took away much of his mobility. Some insiders figured Worthy's injury would cost the Lakers the series. Others figured that without center Kareem Abdul-Jabbar (who had retired after the 1989 season), Los Angeles just wasn't as potent as a playoff team. Game 1, however, seemed to confirm Riley's prediction. The Lakers won, 93-91, on a three-pointer by center Sam Perkins with 14 seconds left in the game. The Bulls got the ball to Jordan, but his 18-foot jumper with four seconds left went in the basket and spun out. It seemed that Jordan was human after all and that the Laker experience just might deliver them.

The Bulls, though, would have none of the conventional thinking. They blew out the Lakers in Game 2, 107-86. The Chicago starters shot better than 73 percent from the floor, with Paxson going eight for eight to score 16 points. "Does Paxson ever miss?" the Lakers' Sam Perkins asked.

Paxson shrugged at reporters' questions and said his job was to hit open jumpers. "When I'm in my rhythm, I feel like I'm going to make them all," he said.

Jordan himself had hit 15 of 18 to finish with 33.

Even with the loss, the Lakers were pleased. They had gotten a split in Chicago Stadium and were headed home for three straight games in the Forum. The pressure was on Chicago.

But the Bulls met the challenge in Game 3. Jordan hit a jumper with 3.4 seconds left to send the game into overtime. There, the Bulls ran off eight straight points for a 104-96 win and a 2-1 lead in the series. Jordan was elated, but he refused to dwell on the victory. The Lakers had plenty of experience in coming back, he said.

Yet experience proved no match for the Bulls' young legs and determination. For Game 4, Chicago's weapon was defense. The Bulls harried the Lakers into shooting 37 percent from the floor. Chicago won, 97-82. The Lakers' point total was their lowest since before the shot clock was adopted in 1954. They managed a total of 30 points over the second and third quarters. Perkins had made just one of his 15 shots.

"I didn't even dream this would happen," Magic said.

But the Bulls did. Suddenly, they were on the verge of the improbable.

"It's no surprise the way they've been defending," Laker coach Mike Dunleavy said of the Bulls. "They are very athletic and very smart."

And very hot.

On the eve of Game 5, Jordan publicly acknowledged the team's debt to Cartwright. "He has given us an edge in the middle," he said. "He has been solid for us. . .This guy has turned out to be one of the most important factors for this ball club, and he has surprised many who are standing here and who play with him."

Told of Jordan's comments, Carwright said, "That stuff really isn't important to me. I've always figured what goes around comes around. What's really important to me is winning a championship."

As Jordan predicted, the Bulls turned to their offense to claim the title in Game 5, 108-101. Pippen led the scoring parade with 32 points, and Paxson did the damage down the stretch, hitting five buckets in the final four minutes to score 20 points and seal the win. Time and again, Jordan penetrated, drawing the defense, then kicked the ball out to Paxson, who hit the open shots. In the bedlam on the Forum floor following the Bulls' 108-101 victory, Laker superfan Jack Nicholson hugged Phil Jackson, and Magic Johnson tracked down Jordan to offer his congratulations. "I saw tears in his eyes," Johnson said. "I told him, 'You proved everyone wrong. You're a winner as well as a great individual basketball player.'"

By the time Jordan squeezed through the crowd to the locker room he was openly weeping. "I never lost hope," he said, his father James and wife Juanita nearby. "I'm so happy for my family and this team and this franchise. It's something I've worked seven years for, and I thank God for the talent and the opportunity that I've had."

"I've never been this emotional publicly," he said. "When I came here, we started from scratch. I vowed we'd make the playoffs every year, and each year we got closer. I always had faith I'd get this ring one day."

The Bulls returned to Chicago and celebrated their championship in Grant Park before a crowd estimated at between 500,000 and a million. "We started from the bottom," Jordan told the screaming masses, "and it was hard working our way to the top. But we did it."

RUNNING THE ROCKY ROAD

Perhaps the most amazing thing about the Bulls' second championship was the amount of discord and controversy they had to overcome to win it. Long-festering resentment surfaced during the 1991 championship celebration when Michael Jordan decided not to join the team in the traditional Rose Garden ceremony with President George Bush. Much of the discord stemmed from the relationship between Horace Grant and Jordan.

"I think it was a situation," Phil Jackson later observed, "where Horace felt demeaned, felt that he was made light of, and he wanted to be a person of importance."

Grant also served as a source for the book, *The Jordan Rules* by *Chicago Tribune* sportswriter Sam Smith. Marketed as the inside story of the Bulls' championship season, the book and its unflattering portraits of Jordan and Jerry Krause rocked the franchise just as the 1991-92 season opened.

"*The Jordan Rules* was very divisive to the team," Jackson said. "But the one great thing about this group of guys. They never let the external stuff bother the team's play on the floor."

THE BIG START

Despite the turmoil, Krause set the roster with a November trade, sending disgruntled Dennis Hopson to Sacramento for reserve guard Bobby Hansen. The Bulls raced out to a 37-5 record including a 14-game winning streak, the longest in team history. They slipped over late January and February, going only 11-8. But by the first of March, the Bulls were back on track and closed out the schedule with a blistering 19-2 run to finish 67-15, the franchise's best record. Jordan claimed his sixth straight scoring crown and won his third league MVP award. He and Pippen were named to the All-Defense first team, and Pippen earned All-NBA second team honors.

"We really had an outrageous year," Jackson said. "We won 67 games, and basically I felt like I had to pull back on the reins, or they would have tried to win 70 or 75. The playoffs were an entirely different story from the regular season. We had injuries, and we had to face New York. And teams were coming at us with a lot of vim and vigor."

In the first round of the playoffs, the Bulls faced the Miami Heat, a 1989 expansion team making its first postseason appearance. Chicago quickly claimed the first two games in the best-of-five series, then headed to Miami for Game 3.

"In Miami's first playoff game ever, it was clacker night,"

recalled Bulls broadcaster Tom Dore. "What they said was, any time Michael gets the ball or shoots a free throw, go nuts with those clackers. Make all kinds of noise. Well, it worked in the first quarter. The Heat had a big lead. And in fact, we were wondering, can the Bulls come back from this? And Michael stopped by the broadcast table and looked at Johnny Kerr and me and said, 'Here we come.' That's all he said. Boy, did he ever. He went absolutely beserk, scored 56 points, and the Bulls won, swept the series."

Jordan always seemed to relish the New York challenge.

KNICKERBOCKER BLUES

Next up were the New York Knicks, now coached by Pat Riley and employing a physical style strikingly similar to the Pistons. The Knicks used their muscle to claim Game 1 in Chicago Stadium. B.J. Armstrong helped even the series at 1–1 by hitting big shots in the fourth quarter of Game 2. Then the Bulls regained the homecourt advantage in Game 3 in New York when Jordan finally broke free of New York's cloying defense for his first dunks of the series.

The Knicks, powered by Xavier McDaniel, fought back to even it with a win in Game 4.

In critical Game 5, Jordan took control by going to the basket. The Knicks kept fouling him, and he kept making the free throws, 15 in all, to finish with 37 points as the Bulls won, 96-88. "Michael is Michael," Riley said afterward. "His game is to take it to the basket and challenge the defense. When you play against a guy like him, he tells you how much he wants to win by how hard he takes the ball to the basket."

The Knicks managed to tie it again with a Game 6 win in New York, but the Bulls were primed for Game 7 in the Stadium and walked to the win, 110-81. "We got back to playing Bulls basketball," Armstrong explained.

They resumed their struggle in the conference finals against the Cavaliers, who managed to tie the series at 2-2, but the Bulls had just enough to escape Cleveland, 4-2. "John Paxson turned to me in the locker room and said, 'What a long, strange trip it's been,'" Jackson confided to reporters. "And he wasn't just quoting the Grateful Dead. It has been a long, strange trip. Last year was the honeymoon. This year was an odyssey."

TITLE TIME NUMBER TWO

The Finals against the Portland Trail Blazers brought more turbulence, which was intermittently calmed by Jordan's memorable performances. The Blazers—driven by Clyde Drexler, newly acquired Danny Ainge, Cliff Robinson, Terry Porter and Buck Williams—answered with a few performances of their own. Ultimately, though, the glory was Jordan's. In Game 1, he scored 35 points in the first half, including a record six three-pointers, enough to bury the Blazers, 122-89.

"The only way you can stop Michael," said Portland's Cliff Robinson, "is to take him off the court."

"I was in a zone," said Jordan, who had focused on extra hours of practice, shooting long range, before Game 1. "My threes felt like free throws. I didn't know what I was doing, but they were going in."

In Game 2, the Blazers' hopes dimmed when Drexler fouled

out with about four minutes left. But they rallied with a 15-5 run to tie the game, then somehow won, 115-104, on the strength of Danny Ainge's nine points in overtime. "Momentum is a fickle thing," Ainge mused afterward.

"It was a gift in our hands and we just gave it away," Horace Grant said.

The Blazers had their split, with the series headed to Portland for three games. But the Bulls' defense and a solid team effort—Pippen and Grant scored 18 each to go with Jordan's 26—ended thoughts of an upset with a win in Game 3, 94-84.

Later, Jackson would explain that the Blazers rushed to take a late flight home after Friday night's Game 2, which cost them important sleep, while the Bulls waited until Saturday to travel. "They controlled the tempo, we shot poorly and never got in the groove," Portland coach Rick Adelman admitted.

Having regained their rest, the Blazers struggled to stay close through most of Game 4, then moved in front with just over three minutes left and won it, 93-88, on a final surge. The outcome evened the series at 2-2.

But Game 5 was another Jordan showcase. Going to the hole repeatedly, he drew fouls and made 16 of 19 free throws to finish with 46 points, enough to give the Bulls a 119-106 win and a 3-2 lead. Again, the Blazers had stayed close, but Jordan's scoring had kept them at bay over the final minutes. His raised clenched fist and defiant grimace afterward served notice to Portland.

Game 6 back in the Stadium should have been a Chicago walk, but the Bulls fell into a deep hole, down 17 points late in the third quarter. Then Jackson pulled his regulars and played Bobby Hansen, B.J. Armstrong, Stacey King and Scott Williams with Pippen. Hansen stole the ball and hit a shot, and the rally was on. Strangely, Jordan was on the bench leading the cheering.

With about eight minutes to go, Jackson sent Jordan back in, and the Bulls powered their way to their second title, 97-93, bringing the Stadium to an unprecedented eruption.

It was Michael versus Clyde Drexler in the 1992 championship series.

GARY GLITTER

"The final against Portland was a dramatic night for us and all Chicago fans," Phil Jackson recalled. "We came from 17 down at the end of the third quarter to win the championship. What followed was an incredible celebration."

"The team had gone down to the dressing room to be presented with the Larry O'Brien trophy by David Stern and Bob Costas," remembered Bulls vice president Steve Schanwald. "Jerry Reinsdorf and Jerry Krause and Phil Jackson and

Michael and Scottie stood on a temporary stage and accepted the trophy. But we didn't have instant replay capability, so the fans were not able to share in that moment. Up in the Stadium, we were playing Gary Glitter on the loudspeaker, and the crowd was just reveling in the championship. It had been a great comeback in the fourth quarter, really initiated by our bench. So the victory was a total team effort.

"I went down and asked Jerry Reinsdorf if we could bring the team back up. He said, 'It's alright with me, but ask Phil.' I said, 'Phil, the fans are upstairs. They're not leaving; they're dancing. We've got to bring the team back up and let them enjoy this thing.' Phil thought for a moment, and Bobby Hansen was standing nearby. Phil asked Bobby what he thought, and Bobby said, 'Let's do it!' Phil has the ability to whistle very loud. He put two fingers in his mouth and whistled over all that noise and champagne and everything. He got everything quieted down. He said, 'Grab that trophy. We're going back up to celebrate with our fans!' With that, Michael grabbed the trophy, and we went back upstairs."

When we started emerging through the tunnel, we started to play the opening to our introduction music. It's very dramatic. It's 'Eye in the Sky' by the Alan Parsons Project. So the crowd knew when the music started playing something was happening. The team came up through the tunnel, and all of the sudden the crowd just exploded. It was a 10,000-goose bump experience.

"All of a sudden some of the players, Scottie and Horace and Hansen, those guys got up on the table so that everybody could see them in the crowd. Then Michael came up and joined them with the trophy, and they started dancing. It was just an electrifying experience, and I think for anybody that was there it was a moment that they will never forget as long as they live."

The team opted for another rally in Grant Park a few days later to rejoice with their fans. Again hundreds of thousands gathered to scream and celebrate. "We will be back," Bill Cartwright promised.

"Let's go for a three-peat," Pippen suggested, and the crowd's roar in response made it clear that no one in Chicago doubted it was possible.

TROUBLE AGAIN

Jerry Krause had hoped that Scottie Pippen and Michael Jordan would decline their invitations to play for the United States on the Dream Team in the Olympic Games in Barcelona over the summer of 1992. Krause wasn't being unpatriotic. He just wanted the Bulls' superstars to rest. They both agreed to the honor, however, and despite the United States' easy breeze to the gold medal that August, both players came home thoroughly tired by the experience.

Horace Grant, who had said many times that no one understood his importance to the Bulls, seemed jilted by the attention showered on Jordan and Pippen. And when Jackson allowed the two stars to take a casual approach to training camp in early October, Grant complained to the media about "double standards" and "preferential treatment."

Later in the season, he would accuse Pippen of arrogance. Ultimately, this sniping would prove to be a minor rift between the two friends, but both agreed that they weren't as close as they had been.

Besides the "divisiveness" that Jackson loathed, the Bulls encountered a rash of physical ailments. Cartwright, 35, and Paxson, 32, had offseason surgery on their creaky knees, and Pippen would be troubled by a bad ankle for most of the season. For Jordan, the pains were first his arch and then his wrist.

B.J. Armstrong, who had long struggled with the Bulls' triple post offense, finally found enough of a comfort level to replace Paxson in the starting lineup.

MORE OF MIKE'S NUMBERS

Ultimately, the Bulls' only real opponent proved to be the sameness. Jordan called it "monotony." For most teams, that might have meant 38 wins. For the Bulls, it meant another divisional championship, 57 wins (their fourth straight 50-win season) and a seventh consecutive scoring crown for Jordan, tying him with Wilt Chamberlain.

On January 8th, Michael scored his 20,000 career point, having reached that total in just 620 games. The only man to do it faster was Wilt Chamberlain, who reached the milestone in 499 games. "It looks like I fell short of Wilt again, which is a privilege," Jordan said. "I won't evaluate this until I'm away from the game. I'm happy about it, but we still have a long season to go. I'm sure as I get older, I'll cherish it more."

In another game, an overtime loss to Orlando, Jordan scored 64 points, although Pippen complained afterward that Jordan had taken too many shots.

GAINS AND PAINS

Jordan would be named All-NBA first team again, and both he and Pippen would make the All-Defense first team. In the 1993 Finals, Jordan would collect an unprecedented third straight MVP award.

For Jackson, December would bring his 200th win, reaching the mark faster than any coach in league history. Even with the accomplishments, it was not a regular season to treasure.

"Guys were hurt," Jackson explained. "Pippen with his ankle, Jordan with his plantar fascia. All of those things prevented us from getting a rhythm. We weren't in great condition. So when practices were done hard and precise, we ended up suffering in our game effort."

"They were tired," recalled Bulls trainer Chip Schaefer. "No question. Michael and Scottie were tired in the fall of '92. That was just a tough, long year, and really a tough year for Michael. It seemed like one thing after another. The press was picking on him, things just happening all year long. As soon as one thing would let up, it seemed like another came into play. There was one book or one incident constantly. It got to be not about basketball, but personal things that really shouldn't have been part of it at all. You could just see it starting to wear on him a little bit. In some private moments, he expressed that. It was really evident that he was getting tired. Tired physically, tired mentally of the whole thing."

Jackson's answer was a series of psychological ploys to motivate his players. "Phil played a lot of mind games," Jordan recalled. "He waged psychological warfare to make you realize the things you have to do to be a winner."

"It's a funny thing to look at the history of the NBA and the way teams kind of rise and fall," Chip Schaefer noted. "For all intents and purposes, it looked like it was going to be New York's year. They paid their dues. The Knicks absolutely destroyed us, beat us by 37 points in late November that year. They played like it was Game 7 in the playoffs. We went in kind of yawning. No big deal. Michael sprained his foot early in the game, and they just crushed us. We still won 57 games that year, but we just kind of floundered."

KNICKED AGAIN

For two years, the New York Knicks had seen their championship hopes end in seven-game playoff battles with the Bulls. With good reason, they figured they needed the homecourt advantage to dethrone Jordan and his teammates. So coach Pat Riley turned the full force of his considerable intensity to driving New York to 60 wins and the homecourt advantage in the Eastern Conference.

The Bulls, meanwhile, slipped quietly into second place and seemed almost distracted heading into the playoffs. But they quickly picked up the pace, sweeping three games from Atlanta in the first round, then devastating the Cleveland Cavaliers again by winning four straight. Jordan capped the series with a last-second game winner in Cleveland that closed the chapter on his domination of the Cavs.

"Once the playoffs rolled around," Schaefer recalled, "Michael managed to turn it on again. But we faced New York again. We didn't have homecourt, so there really wasn't much reason to be optimistic about it."

Jordan loathed the Knicks' brutish style. "They play like the Pistons," he said testily. Perhaps New York's frustration made them worse. Plus Jackson and Riley made no great effort to hide their dislike for one another. In Game 1 in Madison Square Garden, the Knicks banged Jordan into a 10-for-27 shooting performance and won, 98-90. "I told the team I let them down," Jordan said afterward.

The acknowledgment did little good because the same thing happened in Game 2. Jordan missed 20 of 32 shots, and the Knicks won again, 96-91. Afterward, the smugness in New York was tangible. "Now the Bulls are down two games and have to beat the Knicks four games out of five games if they are going to have a chance at three titles in a row," crowed *New York Daily News* columnist Mike Lupica.

A media firestorm then erupted after a *New York Times* report that Jordan had been seen at an Atlantic City casino in the wee hours before Game 2, suggesting that perhaps he wasn't properly rested for competition. The headlines brought Jackson and Krause quickly to his defense. "There is no problem with Michael Jordan," Krause told reporters. "He cares about winning and is one of the great winners of all time."

"We don't need a curfew," Jackson added. "These are adults. . . .You have to have other things in your life or the pressure becomes too great."

With this issue hovering over the events, the series moved to Chicago.

"The Bulls came back for practice at the Berto Center," recalled veteran Chicago radio reporter Cheryl Ray. "I've never seen as much media gathered for an event. Michael stepped out of the training room, and I said, 'Michael would you just go over the chain of events for us? Would you tell us what happened and where this story is coming from?' He did, and then a television newsperson from a local Chicago station started grilling him as though he were an alderman being convicted of a crime. Chuck Gowdy from Channel 7 was saying things like, 'Do you do this before every game? Do you have a gambling problem?' He kept hammering and hammering away, and eventually Michael just shut up and walked away. He didn't talk until the first game against Phoenix."

Jordan ceased speaking with the media, and his teammates followed suit. With Pippen taking charge, the Bulls won big in Game 3 in the Stadium, 103-83.

"The moment I knew we were going to win that series was after Game 3," Schaefer recalled. "After we'd beat them pretty soundly and brought the series back to 2-1, Patrick Ewing made a comment that, 'We don't have to win here in Chicago.' As soon as I heard him say that, I knew we were going to win the series. If you have that attitude, you may lose a game and lose your edge. You can't assume you're going to win all of your home games. It was Scottie who got us that series. He always seemed to have a knack when Michael might have been having a tough time, to step up and do what needed to be done."

Jordan scored 54 points to drive Chicago to a win in Game 4, 105-95, and it was Jordan's triple-double (29 points, 10 rebounds and 14 assists) that dominated the statistics column in Game 5, when Chicago took the series lead, 3-2. But it was Pippen's successive blocks of putback attempts by New York's Charles Smith late in Game 5 in New York that closed off the Knicks' hopes. Then, when the Bulls completed their comeback in Game 6 in Chicago, it was Pippen again doing the final damage, a corner jumper and a trey, in a 96–88 victory.

"This hurts bad," said New York's Doc Rivers when it was over.

John Paxson would hit the winning shot against Phoenix in 1993.

THREE-FEAT

The Bulls had persevered to return to their third straight NBA Finals. This time, Charles Barkley, now with the Phoenix Suns, was the opponent. After several frustrating and troubled years in Philadelphia, Barkley had been traded to the Suns before the

1992-93 season, and like that he was reborn, earning league MVP honors and leading the Suns to the Finals.

The Suns had won 62 games and had the homecourt advantage for their brand new America West Arena. The Bulls, though, had plenty of confidence. They had always done well against Barkley's Philadelphia teams. Pippen's and Grant's defense would shackle him again, and B.J. Armstrong had the quickness to stay with Phoenix point guard Kevin Johnson.

Those plans eventually worked out, but in the short term there was more turbulence ahead. No sooner had Jordan's Atlantic City casino jaunt slipped out of the news than Richard Esquinas, a San Diego businessman, stepped forward with a book claiming that Jordan owed him $1.2 million from high-stakes losses from betting on golf games.

In a taped interview at halftime of Game 1 of the Finals, Jordan answered, admitting that he had lost substantial sums to Esquinas, but nowhere near the figure claimed. Questions about whether this distraction would hinder the Bulls were quickly put aside when Chicago claimed the first game, 100-92. Jordan hit for 31 points, Pippen for 27, while the Bulls' defense harassed Barkley into shooting 9 for 25.

The Suns seemed nervous. And they sank deeper into trouble in Game 2. Barkley and Jordan both scored 42 points, but the Bulls' defense clamped down on Kevin Johnson and Phoenix guard Dan Majerle to take a 2-0 series lead, 111-108. Bulls assistant Johnny Bach had devised a defensive scheme, deployed by Armstrong, that had Johnson talking to himself and sitting much of the fourth quarter.

Suddenly Phoenix faced three games in Chicago and the prospects of a sweep. The Suns answered by scratching out a 129-121, triple-overtime win in Game 3. Kevin Johnson played an NBA-Finals record 62 minutes and scored 25 points with seven rebounds and nine assists. Majerle had scored 28 and Barkley 24.

"I thought it was never going to end," Phil Jackson said afterward.

Sensing a vulnerability in his team, Jordan came on strong in Game 4, scoring 55 points and driving the Bulls to a 108-98 win and a 3-1 series lead. The Suns had allowed Jordan time and again to glide inside for handsome little dunks and bank shots. Phoenix was only down two at the end, but Armstrong's pressure and a key late steal widened the Bulls' lead. Jordan's

Chicago Stadium had been the Bulls home for two decades.

point total tied Golden State's Rick Barry for second place on the all-time single-game list. The record was held by Elgin Bayor, who had scored 61 in a game against Boston in 1962.

The Bulls were up 3-1 with Game 5 on their home floor. However, they strangely teetered at the brink of their accomplishment. Jordan swore to his teammates that he wouldn't accompany them back to Phoenix if they failed to deliver the championship in the Stadium. Regardless, the Bulls stumbled, and the Suns busied themselves with defense. Jordan's easy baskets disappeared as Phoenix congregated in the lane.

With Johnson scoring 25 and Sir Charles 24, the Suns got

the win they needed, 108-98, to return the series back to their home court. There had been speculation that if the Bulls won Game 5 in Chicago, the city would be racked by the riotous celebration that had marred the team's previous championships. In fear of that, many merchants had boarded up their stores.

"We did the city a favor," Barkley said as he left town. "You can take all those boards down now. We're going to Phoenix."

So was Jordan, contrary to his vow, and the Bulls were fighting feelings that they had let their best opportunity slip away.

"Michael seems to sense what a team needs," recalled Bulls broadcaster Tom Dore. "They had just lost. But Michael walked on the plane going to Phoenix and said, 'Hello, World Champs.' He's got a foot-long cigar, and he's celebrating already because he knows the series is over. He knew, going to Phoenix, that they were going to win."

Barkley had claimed that "destiny" belonged to the Suns, but over the first three quarters of Game 6 it seemed the Phoenix players were feeling pressure more than anything else. Meanwhile, the Bulls phalanx of guards, Jordan, Armstrong, Paxson and seldom-used reserve Trent Tucker, fired in nine three-pointers over the first three periods to stake Chicago to a 87-79 lead.

From there, however, it was the Bulls' turn to succumb to the pressure. They missed nine shots and had two turnovers the first 11 times they got the ball in the fourth quarter. The Suns closed within a point, then surged to take a 98-94 lead with 90 seconds left. Then Jordan pulled down a defensive rebound and wound his way through traffic to the other end for a short bank shot. It was 98-96 with 38 seconds to go. Majerle's shooting had helped Phoenix back into the series, but on the Suns' next-to-last possession he shot an air ball.

The Bulls had another chance with 14.1 seconds to go. After a timeout, Jordan inbounded the ball to Armstrong, then got it back and passed ahead to Pippen. The ball was supposed to go back to Chicago's Superman, but Pippen saw that Jordan was covered and motored into the lane, where he was greeted by Suns center Mark West.

Alone on the near baseline was Grant, who had scored a single point in the game, who had had a stickback opportunity moments earlier and almost threw the ball over the backboard. Pippen whipped him the ball, and scrambling out of his personal terror, Grant passed up the shot to send the ball out to John

Paxson, all alone in three-point land to the left of the key.

"I knew it was in as soon as Pax shot it," Jordan said.

Paxson's trey and a key Grant block of Johnson's last shot moments later delivered the Bulls' third championship.

"That's instinct," Paxon said of the shot afterward. "You catch and you shoot. I've done it hundreds of thousands of times in my life. Horace gave me a good pass."

Reporters converged upon Jordan afterward to ask if he planned to retire. "No," he assured them. "My love for this game is strong."

Yet time would reveal it was more than a matter of love. Still the effects of Paxson's big shot and three straight championships would linger sweetly in Chicago.

"It was like a dream come true," Paxson recalled in 1995. "That's the greatest part about winning, is how you feel as a group. You're happy for one another. You look at small plays that happen in a game, the people who come off the bench and provide something that the group needs. You understand how important each individual is to your success. It's not just the best player. It's from one to 12, the coaches included, and your appreciation for each is very high."

MICHAEL JORDAN

CHICAGO BULLS

1984 — 1993

The best there ever was. The best there ever will be.

DEDICATED
NOVEMBER 1, 1994

RETIREMENT

At the close of the 1993 playoffs, Michael Jordan sat atop the NBA mountain. During the Finals, he had averaged 41 points per game, breaking the championship series record of 40.8 points per game set by the Warriors' Rick Barry in 1967.

Yet there was little question among Jordan's close associates that he had grown weary of the grind. In his public comments during the 1993 season, he had made oblique references to retirement. Yet in the locker room victory celebration, Jordan had said he would be back for another campaign come fall.

However, late that July, a dreadful turn of events hastened his departure from the game. Jordan's popular father, James Jordan, was found murdered in South Carolina, ostensibly the victim of a random roadside killing. Yet the news of Mr. Jordan's death was followed quickly by wild speculation that somehow Jordan's golf wagering might be a factor. That, as much as anything, seemed to be the final insult for Jordan. On October 6, 1993, he abruptly announced his retirement from the Bulls.

"That's the paranoia that builds in people's minds and sometimes drives you crazy," Phil Jackson said of the media speculation.

The situation was clearly too much for Jordan to handle, so he came to a quick decision to leave the game, so quick, in fact, that he didn't have time to notify his mother, who was in Africa on a humanitarian mission.

"People were definitely depressed," recalled Bulls vice president Steve Schanwald. "It happened with such suddeness, it was so out of the blue, that it kind of took the wind out of people's sails."

Perhaps the greatest emptiness was felt in the NBA's

◄ Jordan at the unveiling of his statue outside the United Center.

administrative offices, where staff members began trying to figure out how to replace the greatest attraction in basketball history.

Jordan soon announced that he would try his hand at minor league baseball in the Chicago White Sox farm system, with the hopes that he might someday make it to the big leagues.

"Looking back on it, it was a beautiful thing Michael did," Jackson said. "What a risk he took trying to play baseball. The whole idea that he's going to go out and give up everything to try that at his age. That's the wonderful thing about it. Michael is such a special person."

It was this risk-taking nature that made it impossible for the NBA to replace him. The Houston Rockets, however, had no trouble with the circumstances. They took the opportunity to win two championships while Jordan was discovering that he had trouble hitting a curve ball.

Pippen was a rare talent.

PIPPEN SHOULDERS THE LOAD

Jordan's abrupt retirement left Jerry Krause hustling to patch together a replacement combination for the backcourt that included Pete Myers and Ron Harper. There were several other new faces on the roster. After years of trying, Krause had lured Toni Kukoc, the 6-11 Croation, from Europe. Krause had pursued Kukoc since the Bulls drafted him in the second round in 1990.

The general manager had also signed free agent Steve Kerr with the idea that he would eventually replace Paxson. For the frontcourt, Krause signed 7-foot journeyman Bill Wennington and later traded Stacey King to Minnesota for 7-foot-2 Luc Longley.

There was immediate speculation that these newly reconstituted Bulls would fail miserably without Jordan. But just the opposite happened. The coaching staff did perhaps its best job in Jackson's tenure with the team. And Scottie Pippen, Horace Grant and B. J. Armstrong showed that they had developed into outstanding players in their own right. All three were selected for the All-Star team, the first time that three Bulls had been selected.

Amazingly, these Jordan-less Bulls won 55 games and made a strong-but-controversial run into the 1994 playoffs. Their first-round opponents, the Cavaliers, fell easily, leaving the Bulls to face Pat Riley's Knicks in the Eastern semifinal.

PIPPEN JUST SAYS NO

In Game 1 in New York, the Bulls had a 15-point lead but seemed to run out of energy. It was a bitter, frustrating loss, the kind that Jackson feared could do harm to his team. So, instead of practicing, he decided they needed a break, which turned out to be an impromptu ride on the Staten Island Ferry.

It did not, however, bring them a win in Game 2. The Knicks strong-armed a second win, and the series moved to Chicago with the Bulls down 2-0. There, in Game 3, they seemed set to fall off the edge. The Knicks had a one-point lead with 1.8 seconds left. Chicago had the ball and called a time-out, during which Jackson set instructions for the ball to go to

Kukoc for the final shot. Pippen was infuriated. He was the superstar of the team, burdened all season with the load of carrying the Bulls alone. He believed the shot should have been his to take. So he refused to go back in the game. Cartwright was at first stunned, then furious with Pippen.

Nonplussed, Jackson substituted, leaving Pippen on the bench, and Kukoc hit the game-winning shot. The aftermath, however, was soon awash in controversy. Pippen was roundly lambasted for letting his team down in the clutch.

"Those times are the moments in games that you live for," Pippen later explained. "And I thought it was an injustice the way Phil treated me, and I had to say something, right or wrong. So it wasn't what people wanted to hear."

Somehow, the team shook off the incident and claimed a 12-point win in Game 4 to even the series. The Bulls then could have won crucial Game 5 in New York. In the closing seconds, the Bulls had the lead and seemingly the win when referee Hue Hollins whistled Pippen for a late foul on New York's Hubert Davis beyond the top of the key. The Bulls incredulously protested, and supervisor of officials Darrell Garretson later said the call was terrible. But Davis hit the game-winning free throws. Back in Chicago for Game 6, the Bulls played well and evened the series at three-all, only to fall by 10 in Game 7 in New York. In the aftermath, Krause began discussions to trade Pippen.

SINKING

There were major changes in the months leading up to the 1994-95 season. Scott Williams became a free agent and accepted a lucrative offer to play in Philadelphia. Then the re-signing of Horace Grant got mired in dispute, and he left the Bulls to sign with the Orlando Magic. John Paxson retired and Bill Cartwright moved to the Seattle SuperSonics.

These changes meant a substantial struggle over the first months of the 1994-95 season. The on-court battles were made worse by a public dispute between Pippen and management over his efforts to have his multiyear contract renegotiated. The feelings between the forward and Krause had hardened after a summertime deal to trade him to Seattle for power forward Shawn Kemp fell through.

44

By early March 1995, the Bulls were struggling to stay above .500, and speculation abounded that once the season was over Pippen would be shipped to another team. Quite suddenly, the entire picture changed in mid–March, when the good people of Chicago learned that the Jordan era wasn't over after all.

MIKE'S RETURN

Without question, the Bulls were caught off guard by Jordan's decision to abandon his attempts at a professional baseball career. Many people in baseball had questioned his skill level, but no one doubted his work ethic. In his determination to learn to hit big league pitching, Jordan came early and stayed late each day at practice.

But the futility was obvious almost from the start. He was too tall, some said, and presented too big a strike zone. If he was light years away, Jordan, a 32-year-old .200 hitter, certainly didn't have time to waste with the protracted baseball strike that had loomed over the game. Hoping it would soon be resolved, he reported to spring training in Florida only to realize that the feud wasn't going to end anytime soon. Then, he had a misunderstanding with White Sox management over dressing room and parking arrangements. So he packed up and went home.

Within days of his departure from Florida, a Chicago radio station reported that Jordan was secretly working out with the Bulls and contemplating a return to basketball.

On March 10, he announced his retirement from baseball, saying his minor league experience had been powerful because it allowed him to rediscover the work ethic that had made him a great basketball player. "I met thousands of new fans," he said, "and I learned that minor league players are really the foundation of baseball. They often play in obscurity and with little recognition, but they deserve the respect of the fans and everyone associated with the game."

MIKE MANIA

Soon the Bulls confirmed that Jordan was working out with the team, and Jackson revealed that Jordan had actually been contemplating a return since October.

Like that, the situation exploded. Scores of media representatives from the major networks and national publications converged on the Berto Center, the Bulls' practice facility in suburban Deerfield, in anticipation of Michael holding a press conference announcing his return.

Still, Jordan wavered that week, pausing, as he would later explain, to contemplate whether he was returning to basketball out of disappointment over the baseball strike, or if he was in fact returning because he loved the game.

His silence drove reporters and fans alike to distraction, with some callers on Chicago's sports radio talk shows claiming that Jordan was toying with the public.

Meanwhile, *USA Today* reported that the stock value of companies who employed Jordan as a spokesman had zoomed up $2 billion on the various stock exchanges in recent days, leading to further speculation that Jordan was engaged in some kind of financial manipulation.

Finally, on Thursday March 16, Jackson told Jordan not to attend practice that day because the media crowd at the Berto Center had gotten too large. That Friday night, the Bulls capped a three-game winning streak and raised their record three notches above .500 by defeating the Milwaukee Bucks in the United Center.

Early the next morning, the Chicago radio waves were abuzz that Jordan would make his announcement that day, and that he would play Sunday on the nationally televised game against Indiana. Down on LaSalle Street, the managers at Michael Jordan's Restaurant heard the news and decided that they better restock the gift shop yet again. The restaurant's business had been slow in February, but the hint of Jordan's return had turned March into a boom, with crowds packing the place virtually every night.

Other fans gathered at the Jordan statue outside the United Center. Revealed in a nationally televised retirement ceremony in November 1994, the statue had quickly become a hot spot for fans and tourists in Chicago. On this Saturday, as the anticipation grew, small groups were drawn to the statue.

"This is like the Colts returning to Baltimore," said one fan, "with Johnny Unitas as quarterback!"

Over at the Berto Center in Deerfield, crowds of fans and

reporters milled about, with many fans hanging from the balconies and walls of the Residence Inn next door. Nine different TV satellite trucks hovered near the building, waiting to blast the news around the world.

Suddenly, practice was over, and like that, Jordan's burgandy Corvette appeared on the roadway, with him gunning his engine and the fans cheering wildly as he sped off. Next came Pippen in a Range Rover, pausing long enough to flash a giant smile through the vehicle's darkly tinted windows.

Moments later, NBC's Peter Vescey did a standup report outside with the fans rooting in the background. He told the broadcast audience that Jordan was returning, that Jordan would play against Indiana on Sunday. The excitement coursed through the city. Chicago, quipped one radio sportscaster, was in a state of "Jorgasym."

Finally, Jordan broke his silence with a two-word press release, issued through agent David Falk.

"I'm back," he said.

INDY

Jordan did not fly to Indianapolis with the team that Saturday night. A crowd of fans and media gathered at the Canterbury Hotel, awaiting the Bulls' arrival. When a limousine with a police escort pulled up, the crowd surged forward. But out stepped a bride and groom. "Who are these people?" the stunned bride asked her new husband.

The team showed up moments later and was roundly cheered, but there was no Jordan. He flew down the next day on a private jet and arrived at the arena with an armada of limousines carrying his security force of 20 to help hold back the crowds.

Shortly after noon, he emerged with his teammates from the visitors' locker room at Market Square Arena. With his jaws working the gum and his glare policing the roster, Jordan gathered his teammates in a huddle, where they joined hands.

"What time is it?" forward Corie Blount yelled.

"It's game time!" they answered in unison.

With that, the Bulls broke and made their way out into the arena, opening the next chapter in the strange, wonderful saga of Air Jordan.

"He is like a gift from God to the basketball game," Huang Gang, a 21-year-old professional player in Beijing, remarked upon hearing the news. "We try to imitate his ground moves. But you can't copy him in the air. He is unique."

Waiting for the game to begin, Pacers coach Larry Brown quipped that the atmosphere was so zany, it seemed like "Elvis and the Beatles are back."

Jordan's return in 1995 sparked a new level of excitement in Bulls fans.

NUMBER 45

To mark the occasion, Jordan wore jersey number 45, his minor league and junior high number, instead of the number 23 that he had made so famous. Number 23 was the last number his father James saw him compete in, Jordan later explained, and he wanted to keep it that way.

Champion, the sportswear manufacturer that holds the NBA license for jerseys, immediately added an extra shift and began producing more than 200,000 No. 45's for sale around the world.

Jordan played against Indiana like someone who had taken two years off. He made just seven of 28 shots, but his defensive intensity helped the Bulls take the division-leading Pacers to overtime before losing. Afterward, Jordan broke his silence to address the hoopla of the preceding 10 days. "I'm human," he said. "I wasn't expecting this. It's a little embarrassing."

He said he had taken his time evaluating his love of the game and had come to the conclusion that it was real. That, he said, was the reason he returned, not financial considerations.

"I wanted to instill some positives back into this game," he said of his return, indicating his displeasure at some of the NBA's highly paid young players. "There's been a lot of negatives lately, young guys not taking care of their part of the responsibility, as far as the love of the game. I think you should love this game, not take advantage of it. . . be positive people and act like gentlemen, act like professionals."

BACK IN THE GROOVE

Three nights later, he scored 27 points by shooting nine of 17 from the floor in a win over the Celtics at Boston Garden. Next would come a last-second shot for a win against Atlanta, and a 56-point performance against the awestruck Knicks in Madison Square Garden. Between these displays of greatness, he struggled through bouts of very ordinary play. Regardless, in a few short games he had served notice that he was indeed back. Which, in turn, led to a revival of the NBA's fortunes. Sagging television ratings abruptly jumped, and suddenly the whole country was watching Michael Jordan's return.

"Everybody was complaing about the season," Phil Jackson said. "It was a lackluster year. It wasn't any fun. All of a sudden Michael comes back, and suddenly people start paying attention to the NBA."

The circumstances engendered an overwhelming belief among Chicagoans that Jordan was about to perform his grandest miracle of all: He would return after a two-year absence, play just 17 games of the regular season, then lead an undermanned Bulls team into the playoffs to capture a fourth title.

It had all the appeal of a storybook ending, which is what it proved to be. Instead of magic, Jordan's return created mostly unrealistic expectations. The Bulls finished in fifth place in the Eastern Conference and had no home court advantage in the playoffs. Still, they managed to oust the Charlotte Hornets in six games. But it became increasingly obvious that Jordan still lacked the stamina and timing to deliver a miracle.

HELLO, 23

In the second round against the Orlando Magic, the Bulls and Jordan found themselves out of sync, particularly in Game 1 in Orlando when Jordan committed two late turnovers that cost the Bulls the game. From there, Jordan missed shots, made miscues and struggled to find a rhythm. Finally, Jordan donned his old jersey number 23 to get a second win, but the Magic took over from there to claim a 4-2 series victory.

What made the loss worse was that the Bulls' primary executioner was former Bull Horace Grant, who had played power forward on Chicago's three championship team. The same Horace Grant who had frequently clashed with Jordan and later departed the Bulls to join Orlando as a free agent after a nasty public exchange of accusations and insults with Bulls chairman Jerry Reinsdorf.

Grant, who always felt that he had been disrespected during his playing days in Chicago, scored early and often, a performance that further emphasized Chicago's weakness at power forward. The final insult came on the Bulls' home floor, when the young Orlando players hoisted Grant to their shoulders and carried him off in celebration.

The Bulls set about establishing a homecourt advantage in the United Center.

THE NEW HOME

"The day after we were out of it we started planning for next year," Reinsdorf said.

The only acceptable goal would be winning the team's fourth NBA championship in 1996.

One critical aspect of that would be re-establishing a home-court advantage in Chicago. For years, that had been a foregone conclusion when the Bulls played in the creaky old Chicago Stadium, the "Madhouse on Madison," whose thundering crowds and intimidating acoustics had hammered many an

51

opponent into submission. But the Stadium was now headed toward life as a parking lot, having been razed to make way for the United Center, the fancy new $175 million building just across Madison Street.

Brand new when the 1994-95 season opened, the United Center seemed awkward and foreign to Jordan, who had once vowed never to play there. He relented, of course, but didn't like it and quipped that he'd like to "blow it up." The remark was something of a setback to the Bulls administrative staff, who had hoped to establish the United Center as the "New Madhouse on Madison," a snazzier, high-tech version of the old barn. But then the Magic had won two playoff games in Chicago, and those hopes dimmed.

GOODBYE B.J., HELLO RON

If the Bulls hoped to win another championship they would have to find a power forward to strengthen their post play. Plus, they would have to find bigger guards.

With this in mind, the Bulls decided to leave veteran B.J. Armstrong, a fan favorite from the championship years, unprotected in the upcoming expansion draft, and turn the chores over to Ron Harper, the former All-Star originally signed in 1994 to help fill the void created by Jordan's retirement. Harper's bountiful athleticism had declined with a series of knee injuries, but the Bulls figured he still had promise.

Harper had struggled most of the 1994-95 season to get the hang of the complicated triple-post offense, and just when he had started to come around, Jordan returned, taking most of his playing time. Soon the whisper circuit around the NBA had Harper pegged as finished, his legs gone, his game headed for mothballs. The whispers quickly became Harper's motivation to show everybody just how wrong they were about the status of his career.

"I think that we felt as a team that we had something to prove," Harper said later. "And on my own I had something to prove. . . . I trained hard. I felt that last year I definitely didn't have the legs to play the style here. I had to learn that, too."

Jordan faced the same task, rebuilding his conditioning and mindset from the months of basketball inactivity, losing what Reinsdorf called his baseball body for a leaner basketball body. Jordan was scheduled to spend the summer months in Hollywood making "Space Jam," his animated Bugs Bunny film with Warner Brothers.

"He didn't want people to think that his skills were diminished," assistant coach Jim Cleamons said of Jordan. "The man has a tremendous amount of pride."

"The game taught me a lesson in the disappointing series I had last year," Jordan would later say. "It pushed me back into the gym to learn the game all over again."

For the most part, his "gym" would be a temporary floor in the Hollywood studio he occupied while making Space Jam. "I've never seen anybody work harder than Michael Jordan," trainer Tim Grover would later say.

Jordan was nearing his 33rd birthday, trying to prepare himself to face not only the game's talented young players, but the spectre of his own legendary youth. No matter what he did as an aging comeback player, he would have trouble measuring up to the standard he had set from 1986 to 1993, when he lorded over the league.

"I'm the kind of person who thrives on challenges," Jordan explained, "and I took pride in people saying I was the best player in the game.

"But when I left the game I fell down in the ratings. Down, I feel, below people like Shaquille O'Neal, Hakeem Olajuwon, Scottie Pippen, David Robinson and Charles Barkley. That's why I committed myself to going through a whole training camp, playing every exhibition game and playing every regular-season game. At my age, I have to work harder. I can't afford to cut corners."

Rodman brought his own sort of mania to Chicago.

ENTER DENNIS

The Bulls coaches figured that with Jordan back full time, with Pippen, Luc Longley and Toni Kukoc maturing, with Ron Harper refurbishing his game, they had just about all of the major pieces in place, except for one.

"We still needed a rebounder," Jimmy Cleamons said.

Someone to give the roster a nasty factor, someone to play defense and buck up the Bulls' courage, someone to go get the ball when the team needed a tough rebound. In other words, someone like Dennis Rodman, the NBA's resident weird dude.

Rodman had been one of the NBA's great mysteries since the Detroit Pistons first selected him in the second round of the 1986 draft. Although some people in the Pistons' organization would later claim that Rodman was fundamentally troubled, many in Detroit simply saw him as a fun-loving, immature guy who could be surprisingly sweet. One of his favorite pastimes was hanging out with teenagers in mall game rooms (growing up in Dallas he had gotten the nickname "Worm" from his antsiness playing pinball). He was unlike many other NBA players in that he had not come up through the ranks of the great American basketball machine. He had not been on scholarship his entire life, wearing the best shoes and equipment and staying in fancy hotels where the meal checks were always paid. Rodman had missed all of that.

Although his two younger sisters were hoops stars in high school and college, Rodman was only 5-foot-9 when he graduated from South Oak Cliff High School in Dallas, where he grew up. Shy and insecure, he hadn't even played high school basketball. His only prospects after high school were a series of menial jobs. But, miraculously, Dennis grew nine inches in one amazing year. By age 20, he was 6-6 and had outgrown his clothes, leaving his only attire the oversized coveralls from his job washing cars.

It was one of his sisters' friends who got him a tryout at Cooke County Junior College in nearby Gainesville, Texas. He played there briefly, dropped out, then wound up at Southeastern Oklahoma State, where he used his size and quickness to become something of a force in NAIA basketball, averaging nearly 26 points and 16 rebounds over the next three seasons. He led the Southeastern Oklahoma State Savages to a district title and into contention for the NAIA national title, all of which prompted the Pistons to select Dennis with the 27th pick in the 1986 draft, the next giant step in his amazing transformation.

Former Pistons coach Chuck Daly recalled that Rodman's first efforts in training camp were rather disappointing, but he recovered and soon found a place in the league by focusing on playing defense and rebounding. He performed these chores so well that most observers considered him a key factor in the

Pistons claiming back-to-back league titles in 1989 and '90.

Rodman had learned to rely on a natural hyperactivity that supercharged his frenetic playing style. "My friends knew I was hyper. Real hyper," he once said of his days growing up in Dallas. "They knew I wouldn't settle down, I wouldn't sleep. I'd just keep going. And now I just focus my energy in something I love to do. Now, I just play basketball, go out there and have a lot of fun and enjoy."

Rodman moved into the starting lineup for 1989-90 and helped the Pistons to yet another championship. It was during this period, as the Pistons shoved aside Jordan and the Bulls in the playoffs for three straight seasons, that fans in Chicago came to absolutely despise Dennis Rodman, Bill Laimbeer and all the other Piston Bad Boys.

Eventually, however, Detroit's guard-oriented offense declined. The Pistons were swept by Chicago in the 1991 playoffs, and although Detroit made a playoff run in 1992, Daly moved on to coach the New Jersey Nets, leaving Dennis without the fatherly coaching connection he badly wanted. Besieged by personal and off-court problems, Rodman's frustrations built, leading to clashes with Pistons coaches and management.

That October of 1993, the Pistons traded him to the Spurs, thus igniting the next amazing stage in the transformation of Dennis Rodman. From all accounts, he came to San Antonio a changed man. As Rodman explained it, "I woke up one day and said to myself, 'Hey, my life has been a big cycle. One month I'm bleeding to death, one month I'm in a psycho zone.' Then all of a sudden the cycles were in balance."

This new "balance" left him searching through a series of tattoo shops, piercing pagodas, alternative bars and hair salons to find the new Dennis, the one with the electric hair. The old Dennis, however, still played basketball like a wild man.

Jack Haley, a free agent signed as the Spurs' 12th man, was assigned a locker next to Rodman. "He wouldn't even acknowledge I was in the room or shake my hand," Haley recalled, "We sat next to each other for almost three months and never spoke a word."

Haley watched in amazement that winter of 1994 as Rodman moved in and silently took control of the power forward spot in San Antonio. "I figured they were padding his stats," Haley said. "I figured no one could get 20 rebounds a night. So I started counting his rebounds. I'd come to him in a game and say, 'You got 17. You need three more.' Or, 'You need two more.' Or, 'You're having an off night. You only got five.' One game, he said to me, 'How many rebounds do I have?' From there, we developed a slow dialogue."

This casual acceptance somehow accelerated into a full-blown friendship about midway through the season. Indeed, Haley found he could hang rather easily on Rodman's zany planet, among his offbeat circle of friends, including a growing number of celebrities, models, hairdressers, coin dealers and whoever else happened to nudge their way into Rodman's presence.

Rodman seemed intent on living by his own rules, being late to practices and games, wearing bizarre clothing and jewelry in practices and generally violating every team rule. After watching him act up in the 1994 and 1995 playoffs, Spurs management began looking around to trade their Dennis the Menace.

"Everybody in the league was scared to death of Dennis," said Toronto Raptors coach Brendan Malone.

Everybody, that is, except Chicago.

Jerry Krause said he remained interested in Rodman only because of Bulls scout Jim Stack. "Jim Stack came to me early in the summer and asked me to look at Rodman," Krause said. "When I put him off, he finally pleaded with me. He talked me into finding out if all the bad things we had heard were true."

Friends, enemies, former coaches, former teammates, the Bulls contacted a whole group of people in their investigation of Rodman. Chuck Daly told them that Rodman would come to play and play hard.

Yet even after Krause's investigation turned up good news, he and Jackson hesitated before moving forward. After all, Jordan and Pippen had loathed Rodman as a Piston. "When he played in San Antonio, I used to absolutely hate Dennis Rodman," said Bulls gaurd Steve Kerr. Pippen, in particular, held a dislike for Rodman, who had shoved him into a basket support during the 1991 playoffs, opening a gash on Pippen's chin that required stitches. Pippen still had a scar from the incident.

"We could be taking a huge step backwards," Pippen warned.

Jordan and Pippen thought about it, then told Krause to go for the deal, which sent Bulls' longtime backup center Will Perdue to San Antonio for Rodman in early October.

Jackson, who was himself a bit of a rebel as a member of the New York Knicks back in the '70s, grew confident that he could coach Rodman. So the move was made, and as extra insurance for communicating with Rodman, the Bulls signed Haley to a $300,000 contract.

"I understand that they're a little leery and a little cautious of having someone like me in here," Rodman said. "They wonder how I will respond to the team. . . I think Michael knows he can pretty much count on me doing a good job. I hope Scottie feels the same way."

"I think everybody was skeptical of what might happen," recalled John Paxson, a Bulls assistant coach that season. "But we were also optimistic as to what could happen. The optimism stemmed from Phil's personality. We felt that if there was anyone around the league who could get along with Dennis and get Dennis to respect him as a coach, it would be Phil."

CHEMISTRY

With his offseason work, Jordan seemed like his former self on the floor. Pippen, too, seemed more at ease with Michael back. Jackson noticed that he seemed more focused than ever.

At center Luc Longley seemed eager to face the challenge of the coming season as a starter, and veteran Bill Wennington was comfortable in his role as a backup. Krause had also brought in guard Randy Brown to work with Steve Kerr as backcourt reserves. Also coming off the bench were Jud Buechler, Dickey Simpkins, and first-round draft pick Jason Caffey out of the University of Alabama

One bubble in the mixture was Toni Kukoc's reluctance to play the sixth man, or third forward. He wanted to start, instead of coming off the bench, but his role in the lineup had gone to Rodman. Jackson talked to Kukoc about the success that Celtic greats Kevin McHale and John Havlicek had enjoyed as sixth men, but it was not a concept that Kukoc embraced immediately.

The other big question was Rodman. Early on, his behavior had been strange but acceptable. But how long would it last?

Rodman was obviously thrilled to be a Bull. "People have to realize that this team is going to be like a circus on the road," he said. "Without me, it would be a circus. But Michael, Scottie and me, it's more of a circus. A lot of people want to see the Bulls again."

Indeed, Rodman's presence made the Bulls even more of a magnetic attraction, if that was possible. Yet, where Jordan and Pippen had always taken a businesslike approach to winning, Rodman brought a fan-friendly, interactive, fun-filled style to the game that always seemed to set any arena on edge. What was he going to do next? That was the question in everyone's mind.

Rodman admitted that even he didn't know sometimes.

"The very first preseason game of the year," Jack Haley recalled, "Dennis goes in the game, Dennis throws the ball up in the stands and gets a delay-of-game foul and yells at the official, gets a technical foul. The first thing I do is I look down the bench at Phil Jackson to watch his reaction. Phil Jackson chuckles, leans over to Jimmy Cleamons, our assistant coach, and says, 'God, he reminds me of me.'"

Reporters and observers began noting that Jackson, who was sporting a beard grown during the offseason, seemed to be taking a more relaxed approach to the game.

"Somewhere about the middle of training camp I realized I was having a lot of fun coaching this team," Jackson later explained, "and Dennis Rodman to me brings a lot of levity to the game. I mean, I get a kick out of watching him play. . . He's such a remarkable athlete and has ability out there. There are some things about his individuality that remind me of myself. He's a maverick in his own way."

ACTION JACKSON

Even before he became the coach of the Chicago Bulls in 1989, Jackson had a well-earned reputation around the NBA as an eccentric. He had a past in Sixties' counterculture, but rather than put it behind him like any other self-respecting yuppie, Jackson gloried in it. He burned incense in his coaching office, practiced meditation, rode a motorcycle, mixed Zen and Native American philosophy with proverbs from his fundamentalist

Christian upbringing, and clung to the Greatful Dead, Timothy Leary and other icons of the period, all to the great amusement of the media, the fans and even his players.

Yet it would be a mistake to assume that Jackson's eccentricities were merely something he did for effect. They lay at the heart of philosophical beliefs he held dearly.

Asked about Jackson early in the year, Rodman said, "Well, he's laid back. He's a Deadhead." Rodman laughed hard at this assessment, and when a reporter asked, "Is he your kind of coach?" he replied, "Oh yeah. He's fancy-free, don't give a damn. With him it's just, 'Go out there and do the job, and let's go home and have a cold one.'"

The results, perhaps, provide the greatest testimonial. The 1995-96 season marked his seventh consecutive campaign coaching the Bulls, the second longest tenure in one job among the NBA's 29 coaches. He had survived those things by overcoming the elements that had made casualties of many of his peers—the exhausting grind of the 82-game schedule, the daily practices, the shuffling and reshuffling of priorities, and always the pressure to win. Jackson's simple answer had been to find his sense of self elsewhere. "Sometimes," he explained, "I think you have to jump off the treadmill, step back a little ways from it, relook it and rethink it."

If that meant preaching to his players about the great white buffalo or giving them obscure books to read or having them pause amid the looniness of the NBA for a meditation session, so be it. On more than one occasion, Jackson's approach has left his players shaking their heads in amusement. "He's our guru," Michael Jordan quipped when asked about Jackson's quirkiness in early 1996. "He's got that yen, that Zen stuff, working in our favor."

While his players didn't accept each and every of his unconventional remedies, they showed an utter and complete faith in him. "I think Phil really has given me a chance to be patient and taught me how to understand the supporting cast of teammates and give them a chance to improve," Jordan said.

"He's an interesting guy," Steve Kerr said of Jackson. "He keeps things very refreshing for us all season. He keeps things fun. He never loses sight of the fact that basketball is a game. It's supposed to be fun. But at the same time, this is our job, too, and he doesn't let us forget about that either."

That's not to say that Jackson would hesitate to get in a player's face, Kerr added. "But when he does it you know it's not personal. That's his strength. He always maintains authority without being a dictator. And he always maintains his friendship without kissing up. He just finds that perfect balance, and because of that he always has everybody's respect. And ultimately that's the hardest part of being a coach in the NBA, I think, is having every player's respect."

"A lot of people say Michael really runs the Bulls," observed John Salley, a late-season addition to the team. "But Phil runs this team. He runs the squad. He runs practice. He runs the film sessions. He splices the film. He organizes practice. He dissects the other team we're playing against. He knows his stuff.

"He's a great coach. He laughs and smiles at life."

MIKE'S MONKEY

It was during the preseason that veteran *Sun Times* columnist Lacy J. Banks predicted the Bulls would win 70 games, which brought hoots of derision. But the seed had been planted.

As if Jordan needed any more motivation.

He had returned in the spring of 1995 to find a Bulls roster of new faces. And that had proved to be almost as much of an adjustment as his conditioning. Jordan seemed closer to Pippen, but his relationships with his newer teammates seemed strained. Some of them thought he was aloof, unless they happened to elicit his competitive anger. Then they felt a singe.

"He knows he intimidates people," Jackson said of Jordan. "I had to pull him in last year when he first came back. He was comfortable playing with Will Perdue. . . He was tough on Longley. He would throw passes that, at times, I don't think anybody could catch, then glare at him and give him that look. And I let him know that Luc wasn't Will Perdue, and it was all right if he tested him out to see what his mettle was, but I wanted him to play with him because he had a big body, he wasn't afraid, he'd throw it around, and if we were going to get by Orlando, we were going to have to have somebody to stand up to Shaquille O'Neal."

Jordan listened. His restraint with teammates, and his unique commitment, would amaze the many witnesses to his 1995-96 performances, beginning with the very first tipoff. He scored 42 points on opening night in a victory over the Charlotte Hornets at the United Center, setting in motion a momentum that would carry his team to five straight wins, the best start in Bulls' history. It quickly became a season of great momentum, with the Bulls seemingly setting a new record each week. Yet the opening night outburst was a message: I'm all the way back.

QUICK START

No sooner had Rodman started to settle in with the Bulls than a calf muscle injury sidelined him for a month.

Even with Rodman out of the lineup, Jordan continued on his tear, scoring big numbers to drive Chicago to five quick wins. Then came a loss to Orlando. The Bulls responded with two quick wins back in Chicago before scorching through a western road trip, winning six of seven games.

On December 2, they closed out the trip at a sizzling 6-1, with Jordan scoring 37 points in a win over the Los Angeles Clippers. "I feel I'm pretty much all the way back now as a player," Jordan said. Indeed, his shooting percentage, a stellar .511 prior to his return, had dipped to just .411 during his 17-game run over the spring of 1995. Now, it had jumped to .493. His scoring, too, was headed back up to a 30-point average from the nine-year low of 26.9 in 1995.

"He's right where I knew he'd be about now," Ron Harper told the writers covering the team. "And that's leading the league in scoring and pulling away from the pack. He's removing every shadow of a doubt that he's the greatest player of all time."

"I'm old," Jordan admitted. "Agewise, I think I'm old. But skillwise, I think I'm still capable of playing the type of basket-ball I know I can play."

THE BIG RUN

The Bulls finished November with a 12-2 record. Then December passed at 13-1. With each victory, speculation mounted as to whether Chicago could win 70 games, breaking the all-time record for wins in a season, set by the 1972 Los Angeles Lakers with a 69-13 finish.

When the Bulls burned their way through January at 14-0, Jackson began talking openly of resting players just to lose a few games and slow things down. In other words, he was worried that his team would get so drunk with winning during the regular season that they wouldn't play sharp ball in the playoffs.

WORM TURNS

After missing time with injury, Rodman came back strong. With his constantly changing hair colors, his raving style, diving for rebounds, challenging opponents, piping off outbursts of emotion, he was creating one funny circumstance after another. Each night he would cap off his performance by ripping off his jersey and presenting it to someone in the home crowd.

"I think they like me," Rodman said of the fans in the United Center.

With this strange chemistry, the juggernaut pushed on, cruising through February at 11-3, and although March was interrupted by a Rodman outburst after which he was suspended for six games for head-butting an official, the Bulls still finished the month at 12-2.

They reached win number 70 in Milwaukee on Tuesday April 16 and closed the regular season with a road win in Washington for a 72-10 finish. From there, Jackson refired the engines for an astounding playoff push.

THE DRIVE

The Miami Heat fell in the first round in three quick games. Then came a grunting rematch with the Knicks, who managed an overtime win at home before stepping aside, 4-1. Next was the rematch the Bulls had waited a whole year for—the Orlando Magic in the conference finals.

To prepare his team, Jackson spliced shots of "Pulp Fiction," the story of two hired assassins, into the scouting tapes of Orlando. The message was clear. He wanted the Bulls playing like killers, which they did. Rodman held Horace Grant scoreless for 28 minutes of Game 1, until the Orlando forward injured his shoulder in the third quarter. What followed was a rash of injuries, and the Magic went poof in four straight games.

"He's the baddest dude to ever lace up a pair of sneakers," Orlando's Nick Anderson said of Jordan after he scored 45 points in Game 4 of the Eastern Conference finals to complete the Bulls' playoff sweep of the Magic.

Ron Harper was a huge, but quiet factor in the Bulls' 1996 championship run.

The 1996 NBA Finals opened on Wednesday, June 5, with the Bulls as 10-1 favorites over the Seattle SuperSonics, who had won an impressive 64 games during the regular season.

As with every other Bulls' opponent, Seattle's big concern was holding back Jordan, who was asked by reporters if he could still launch the Air raids that made him famous. "Can I still take off? I don't know," he said. "I haven't been able to try it because defenses don't guard me one-on-one anymore. But honestly, I probably can't do it. . . I like not knowing whether I can do it because that way, I still think I can. As long as I believe I can do something, that's all that matters."

The Sonics opened the series with 6-10 Detlef Schrempf playing Jordan, but when Michael posted up, guard Hersey Hawkins went immediately to the double team. Seldom one to force up a dumb shot, Jordan found Harper for an open three, and the 1996 Finals were off and running.

Longley used his size to power in 12 first-half points, with the Sonics obviously intent on forcing Jordan to pass. Pippen and Harper both found their offense, leading to Chicago opening an 11-point lead by the third quarter.

The Sonics had seemed to drag a bit, the obvious aftereffects of their seven-game series with Utah in the Western finals, but they found their legs and pulled to 69-67 as the fourth quarter opened. It was then that Toni Kukoc, injured and in a slump for much of the playoffs, regained his form and scored 10 straight points in the first five minutes of the quarter.

"I was waiting for just one good game to come," he said.

To go with his scoring, the Bulls turned on their pressure, forcing seven turnovers in the fourth quarter alone, and won big, 107-90. Jordan topped the Bulls with 28 points, but Seattle's defensive effort had meant that his teammates got off to a good championship start. Pippen scored 21, Kukoc 18, Harper 15 and Longley 14.

Rodman finished with 13 rebounds and watched as the officials ejected Seattle reserve Frank Brickowski for a dubious attempt to engage him in a scuffle, a silly little ploy played out before the network cameras.

The circumstances left Karl furious. "Dennis Rodman is

laughing at basketball," the Seattle coach said before Game 2. "It's silly to give him any credibility for what he does out there."

"A lot of people don't give me enough credit for being an adult," Rodman replied. "Yesterday was a perfect example that I can be under control."

Rodman answered with a 20-rebound performance in Game 2, including a record-tying 11 offensive rebounds that helped Chicago overcome 39 percent shooting. Rodman's total tied a Finals record set by Washington's Elvin Hayes in 1979.

Although he struggled, Jordan willed 29 points into the baskets. And the defense forced another 20 Sonics turnovers, including a batch during a three-minute stretch of the third period, when Chicago pushed the margin to 76-65. Once again, it was Kukoc off the bench contributing the key offense. He hit two three-pointers. Then Pippen got a breakaway jam after a steal, which was followed by a Kukoc slam on a pass from Jordan, whose anger had prompted the outburst in the first place.

"Are you scared?" he had asked Kukoc. "If you are, then sit down. If you're out here to shoot, then shoot."

Kukoc did, and the run provided enough margin for the Bulls to withstand a fourth-quarter Sonics surge. They closed the gap to 91-88, but Rodman got a rebound on a Kerr miss and later hit a big free throw, allowing the Bulls to escape, 92-88.

Harper, the key to Chicago's pressure defense, had reinjured his creaky knee, requiring that fluid be drawn off just before the game. That allowed him to play and contribute 12 points and key defense, but it also meant that he would miss all or most of the next three games.

Karl found himself having to acknowledge just how important Rodman was to Chicago. "He's an amazing rebounder," the Sonics coach said. "He was probably their MVP tonight."

With Harper's knee hurting, the Bulls figured they were in for a fight with the next three games in Seattle's Key Arena. But the Sonics were strangely subdued for Game 3. With Kukoc starting for the injured Harper, the Bulls were vulnerable defensively. But Chicago forced the issue on offense from the opening tip. With Jordan scoring 12 points, the Bulls leaped to a 34-12 lead by the end of the first quarter. For all intents and purposes, the game was over. By halftime, Chicago had stretched the lead to 62-38, and although Seattle pulled within a dozen twice in the third, the margin was just too large to overcome. The second half was marked by Rodman's smirking antics that once again brought the Sonics' frustrations to the boiling point. Brickowski was ejected for a flagrant foul with six minutes left, and the Key Arena fans, so rowdy in earlier rounds of the playoffs, witnessed the display in numbed silence.

Jordan finished with 36 points, but the big surprise was 19 from Longley, who had struggled in Game 2. Asked what had turned the big center's game around, Jackson replied, "Verbal bashing by everybody on the club. I don't think anybody's ever been attacked by as many people as Luc after Friday's game. Tex gave him an earful, and Michael did, too. I tried the last few days to build his confidence back up."

Apparently it worked because Longley's size was one of several elements of the Bulls' attack that troubled the Sonics. Both Pippen and Kukoc responded with solid floor games. Pippen had 12 points, nine assists and eight rebounds, while Kukoc finished with 14 points, seven rebounds and seven assists.

"I saw Chicago with killer eyes," Karl lamented.

"These guys, once they get the grasp on a team, seem to be able to keep turning the screws down more and more," Jackson agreed, adding that his team reminded him of the 1973 New York Knicks team he played on. "They didn't personally like each other as friends, but they liked to play ball together," Jackson recalled. "This group reminds me of that group. . .

"They're not that close, and they're not that distant. They respect each other, and that's the most important thing, especially at this level, when guys are working in this type of business, an entertainment business, where they're vying for glory and fame and commercial success. Guys understand and respect each other's game and territory. Michael and Scottie have given credence to Dennis' commercial avenue that he runs down, and they've all sort of paid homage to Michael and his icon that he carries. And Scottie's been able to take this team and do things as a leader that are very important for us. And there's plenty of room for guys who have an international appeal like Toni Kukoc and Luc Longley. Those things have all worked very well together."

With the victory, the Bulls were up 3-0, on the verge of a sweep that would give them a 15-1 run through the playoffs, the most successful postseason record in NBA history.

ESPN analyst Jack Ramsay, who had coached the '77 Trail Blazers to an NBA title and served as general manager of Philadelphia's great 1967 team, said the Bulls just might be the greatest defensive team of all time. "The best defenders in the game are Pippen and Jordan. . .," he said. "They're just so tough. In each playoff series, they take away one more thing from the opponent, and then you're left standing out there naked, without a stitch of clothes. It's embarrassing."

Harper had vowed he would be able to play in Game 4, and sure enough, he was in the starting lineup. But his knees allowed him no more than token minutes, which left a huge gap in the Bulls' pressure.

It took the Sonics a few minutes to discover this. They missed their first four shots, but a Kemp slam at 9:26 finally awakened the Seattle crowd. The outcome was really settled by a second quarter blitz from which Chicago never recovered. The run would take Seattle to a 36-21 lead. The Bulls pushed back as Jordan furiously berated both his teammates and the officials, but without Harper, the defense offered no real pressure.

The fourth period brought more of the same, which Jackson witnessed morosely, chin in palm. Midway through the quarter, Jordan was called for a double dribble. Furious, he stomped his foot, obviously rattled. He left the game minutes later, having hit just six of 19, and barked furiously from the bench in the closing minutes, with Pippen laughing, squeezing his shoulder, trying to calm him.

For Game 5, Harper was unable to go once again, which put Kukoc in the lineup. The Bulls struggled to play well, but again had no pressure in their defense. The Sonics had only two unforced turnovers at halftime.

With eight minutes to go, Pippen put home a Randy Brown miss to pull to 71-69, but the Sonics answered with an 11-0 run that the Bulls couldn't answer. Up 80-69, the Sonics crowd pushed the decibel level above 117. On the floor, a fan held up a sign that said, "Dennis' Departure Will Leave Us Sleazeless in Seattle."

Rodman showed his anger when Jackson replaced him with Brown; Haley tried to calm him, but Rodman knocked his hand away. Jordan and Pippen, too, had shown flashes of anger, and the media that had been ready to crown them just two days earlier began noting that the Bulls seemed fragmented and tired.

Finally, it ended, 89-78, and for the second straight game, the arena air glittered with golden confetti. The series, miraculously, was returning to Chicago. "The Joy of Six," the Seattle newspapers declared the next day in a headline.

"It's all on them now," Seattle's Gary Payton said.

FATHER'S DAY

Game 6 was played on Father's Day, June 16th, and Jordan felt the rush of emotion, much of it stemming from thoughts of James Jordan, his friend and advisor. "He's always on my mind," Jordan said.

As introductions were set to begin, a loud prolonged applause spread across the United Center, bringing the fans to their feet to pound out the noise. The very mention of the Sonics brought a deep and troublesome boo.

"Ahhnnnd Nooww," announcer Ray Clay began the introductions, but you could hear no more after the 24,000 saw that Ron Harper was in the lineup.

With Harper back, the Bulls' pressure returned, and they picked the Sonics clean time and again. On the day, Harper would play 38 minutes, and when he paused, an assistant trainer would coat his knee with a spray anesthetic. Spurred by his presence, Pippen pushed the Bulls out of the gate in the first period with seven points and two steals, giving Chicago a 16-12 lead.

The Bulls used more of the same to extend the lead in the second, as Jackson leaned back in his seat with his arms folded. Fifty feet away, Karl strolled the baseline, downcast, his hands jammed in his pockets. The lead moved to 27-18 on another Pippen steal and dish to Jordan, but the Sonics pushed right back, moving to 31-27 on a Kemp jam.

Another run by the Bulls punched it back up to 41-29, then Seattle answered again, pulling to 45-38 at the half.

The Bulls, though, saved their killer run for the third, a 19-9 spurt capped by Pippen dishing to Rodman on the break, with the Worm flipping in a little reverse shot as he got fouled, then jutting his fists skyward, bringing yet another outburst from the building, which got louder yet when Rodman made the free throw for a 62-47 lead.

Just when it seemed they would be run out of the building, the Sonics responded with a 9-0 run. To turn Seattle back, Kerr launched a long three, and the Bulls ended the third period up nine, 67-58. With Jordan facing double teams and his own rush of emotions, at least some of the momentum would come from Kukoc, who canned a three from the corner to push it to 70-58.

Later, Kukoc would knock down another trey, for a 75-61 lead. Rodman, meanwhile, was on his way to grabbing 19 rebounds, including another 11 offensive to tie the record that he had just tied in Game 2. Then Longley tried to slam, drew Kemp's sixth foul, and made two free throws to jack the score to 79-65. Pippen followed that with a deep trey, and the party atmosphere rumbled. Kerr hit a jumper to drive it to 84-68 at 2:44, and the whole building was dancing to "Whoop, There It Is!" Yes, there it was, the sweet conclusion to this Great Bull Run, with the Luvabulls wiggling during a timeout, the building hopping, the scoreboard flashing. . .

The dagger, Pippen's final trey on a kickout from Jordan came at 57 seconds, and moments later, the last possession of this very historic season, Jordan dribbling near midcourt, then relinquishing to Pippen for one last delerious airball.

DELIRIUM NUMBER FOUR

As soon as it was over, Jackson stepped out to hug Pippen and Jordan, who broke loose to grab the game ball and tumble to the floor with Randy Brown. Then Jordan was gone, the game ball clutched behind his head, disappearing into the locker room, trying to escape the NBC cameras, searching for haven in the trainer's room, weeping on the floor in joy and pain over his memories on Father's Day.

"I'm sorry I was away for 18 months," he would say later after being named Finals MVP. "I'm happy I'm back, and I'm happy to bring a championship back to Chicago."

"I think we can consider ourselves the greatest team of all time," Pippen said with satisfaction.

Strangely, it was Karl who put the whole show in perspective. "This Bulls team is like the Pistons or Celtics, or some team from the '80s," he said. "This is the '90s, but they play with a learned mentality from an earlier time. This an old-time package.

"I don't know about the Bird Era or the Magic Era. They were great teams, but this Bulls team has that same basic mentality. I like their heart and I like their philosophy."

The circumstances had Jordan already gazing into the future. "Five is the next number," he said with that smile.

fter stacking up the first 70-win season in National Basketball Association history in 1995-96, the Bulls made another run at big numbers in 1996-97.

The season was something of a gamble for the organization. Jerry Reinsdorf had agreed to plunk down a league-record $57 million payroll to see if his club could win its fifth championship in seven years. The biggest chunk of that money was going to Jordan in a $30 million, one-year deal, while Rodman pulled down nearly $10 million himself.

Reporters wondered if the one-year contracts given to Jordan, Rodman and Jackson would undermine the Bulls' chemistry. "A lot of times in this modern-day game, people relax because they know they're going to be around for three or four years," Jordan said as the exhibition season opened. "I think what we're showing is that we're going to play for the moment. We're gonna come out here and play each and every game like it's our last."

Proving Jordan's point, the Bulls rolled out to the best start in franchise history, eviscerating 12 straight opponents. Jordan gave the blastoff a little extra push by zipping Miami for 50 points the third game of the season.

Most of the games weren't even close.

"They're just smart," Seattle forward Shawn Kemp said of the Bulls. "They have a team where they don't make a lot of mistakes. They don't win off true athletic ability. They win off true intelligence."

The streak followed the Bulls' familiar pattern of the previous season. They often toyed with a team early, then selected some point, usually in the second or third quarter, to break the opponent down with pressure defense. "It's definitely satisfying to come out every night and feel like we dismantle people at some point in the game," said Chicago center Luc Longley.

The sign was a certain look of defeat in opponents' eyes, usually after Jordan made a shot and gave them a smile or a wink, which talked louder than trash.

"I see that almost every night," Longley said.

Asked about the look of defeat in the other team's eyes, Jordan replied, "Sure. You can tell." Asked if he ever thought about pitying any of his victims, Jordan quickly said, "No pity. We just want to go out and keep this going. We go out with the motivation that each team is trying to take something from us."

Rodman had troubles aplenty down the stretch in 1997.

The success was all the more remarkable considering Rodman's pronounced ambivalence. No sooner had talk of bettering last season's record-breaking 72-10 season started to get serious than trouble struck. The team suffered its first loss in a road game at Utah where Rodman was badly outplayed by Karl Malone and cost the Bulls the game with a key late technical for shoving Jeff Hornacek. Afterward, Rodman said he had been bored by the proceedings.

A few nights later, the Bulls nearly suffered a second loss to the Los Angeles Clippers when forward Loy Vaught made Rodman look bad. "If we win it again, I'll come back," Dennis said afterward, while wearing pink suede shoes and a blue suede jacket. "If we don't, I'm getting out. I've already made my mark in this game. I've got other things to do."

That same week the pressure on Rodman increased dramatically when Bulls center Luc Longley left Jackson and his teammates furious after he injured his shoulder while bodysurfing in California and was lost for a long stretch of games.

The Bulls returned home to face their second loss of the season, to the Miami Heat, who erupted in ecstatic celebration on the United Center floor. "We'll have that memory," Jordan promised afterward.

In a loss the next night in Toronto, Rodman couldn't keep up with Raptors forward Popeye Jones and was ejected late in the game for disputing an offensive foul call. Afterward, in a lockeroom interview with the Sports Channel, Rodman spewed out a profanity-laced invective against the officials and league commissioner David Stern.

The Bulls responded by suspending Rodman two games, costing him approximately $104,000 in earnings (subtracted from his $9 million salary). Rodman took the news well. "I apologize to all the people, the kids who heard all that," he said.

But there were more danger spots ahead. In January, he kicked a courtside cameraman in the groin in Minneapolis, a move that brought an 11-game suspension and more than a $1 million in fines and lost income. Jordan and Pippen had never hesitated to express their displeasure with Rodman's misbehavior, but the kicking incident brought a strong reaction from teammates and fans. Rodman would have to straighten up or leave the team for good.

STREAKING

The Bulls, meanwhile, had continued to prosper without Rodman's full attention. They racked up a 15-1 November, sank to 11-4 in December, then charged right back with a 13-1 record in January.

The highlights of the first half of the season included Jordan's 51 points against the Knicks in January after New York coach Jeff Van Gundy said Jordan befriended players on opposing teams to defuse their competitiveness. The allegation infuriated Michael, and he answered with the kind of performance that New Yorkers have come to know all too well.

Another highlight was a December overtime win over the Lakers in the United Center. Los Angeles had dominated Chicago through three quarters, building a fat lead until the Bulls' pressure defense began forcing Laker turnovers in the fourth quarter and Toni Kukoc got hot from three-point range. His 31 points allowed the Bulls to tie it at the buzzer, then break it open 129-123 in overtime, leaving the young Lakers aching and embarrassed.

At the All-Star festivities in Cleveland, the league celebrated its 50th anniversary by honoring the 50 greatest players in NBA history at halftime. Jordan and Pippen were among those selected, and Jackson was picked for the list of the league's 10 best coaches.

To emphasize his standing, Jordan finished the game with the first triple-double in All-Star game history. Added to Chicago's loot was Steve Kerr's win in the three-point shootout.

That success, plus the return of Longley and Rodman, helped push the Bulls on another big win streak coming out of the break. The stretch included a career-high 47 points by Scottie Pippen against Denver.

Steve Kerr hit the big shot in 1997.

CRAZY DAZE

March brought its own sort of madness for the Bulls, beginning with Kukoc's foot injury on the third and closing with a knee injury on the 27th that caused Rodman to miss the remainder of the regular season.

In between, the team still managed to roll up a 12-2 record, relying on the emergence of reserve forward Jason Caffey and the usual brilliance of Pippen and Jordan.

The Bulls, though, closed out the last week of the season in a strange funk. Pressing to win 70, the Bulls instead lost three of their last four regular-season games (to finish 69-13) and looked like anything but a team poised to win a championship.

Jackson figured the Bulls lacked "togetherness." Their usually excellent chemistry had finally gone foul with the struggles of an injury-riddled season. Jackson decided to address it with the film clips he spliced into the team's video scouting reports on the postseason. Each playoff season he liked to break the monotony of the team's film sessions by splicing in non-basketball material, which he would use to stress a basketball message.

In 1996, he had used the film "Pulp Fiction," about hired assassins, because he wanted to boost the Bulls' killer instinct.

This time around, he chose "What About Bob," starring Bill Murray as a wacko mental patient who tried to move in with his psychiatrist.

"Every time he used game clips, he'd put in pieces of the movie," Wennington, who missed the playoffs with a foot injury, said of Jackson. "Basically we saw the whole movie. He was implying that we got to come together, that we got to use baby steps to move along and start playing well."

To help emphasize his basketball messages, Jackson also included clips of old Three Stooges movies.

"Tex Winter likes to sing a song when we get together for our morning sessions," Wennington explained. "He likes to sing, 'It's time we get together. Together. Together. It's time we get together. Together again.' That's part of the message. We need to stay together as a team."

Another factor eating at the team's togetherness was the questions about the future hanging over the heads of Jordan, Jackson and Rodman, all on one-year contracts. Would they be back with the Bulls for another season? There was gigantic speculation on this issue in the Chicago press, and the uncertainty tugged at the entire team's peace of mind.

"Phil is the kind of guy who has the ability to not let things distract him," Tex Winter said. "My Lord, I couldn't do it. If I were the head coach, I'd be a maniac by now. And my whole team would be out of whack. That's Phil's strength. This

Rodman thing, all the things that come down along these lines, Phil kinda just handles it in a very natural, easy way."

Jackson was a master at pulling all the disparate elements together. Perhaps there was no better example of this than the team's late-season signee, Brian Williams. He, too, was a free agent, but salary cap restrictions and league compensation rules virtually assured that he would have to move on to another team at the end of the season. Never one to show a fondness for coaches (he had played for four different teams in his six-year career), he had nonetheless taken an immediate shining to Jackson.

"In my time in the league, he's the most thorough, the most understanding coach I've been around," Williams said.

THE DRIVE FOR FIVE

The Bulls opened the '97 playoffs by ditching the Washington Wizards in three quick games in a series highlighted by Jordan scoring 55 points in Game 2. Washington came out strong and caught all of the Bulls blinking, except for Jordan, who proceeded through the evening like he was conducting a shooting drill in solitude. Jumper after jumper after bank shot after dunk after jumper. He made them from all over the floor, while the rest of his teammates seemed to stand transfixed.

With five minutes left in the game, Jordan drove and scored, pushing Chicago up by three. Moments later he got the ball back, motored into the lane, and flexed a pump fake that sent the entire defense flying like some third-world air force. As they settled back to earth, he stuck yet another jumper and followed it on the next possession with a drive that ended in a falling-down, impossible shot from the right baseline that pushed the lead to seven and his point total for the evening to 49.

Michael then wrapped up a 55-point night (the eighth time in his career that Jordan had scored better than 50 in a playoff game) with two free throws that provided Chicago with a 109-104 win and a 2-0 series lead.

"He's the king of basketball," Washington assistant Clifford Ray said afterward. "He's 34 years old, but he still knows and understands 'Attack!' better than anybody in the game. He attacks all the time. He just kept churning away."

Luc Longley said Jordan's conditioning alone was astounding in that it allowed him to score and play intensely active defense over 44 minutes. "These are the games where he demonstrates who he really is," the center added. "Those performances you definitely marvel at. What I marvel at is how many of them you see a year. Perhaps he only had three or four 50-point games this year, but the 30- and 40-point games he has almost every night. The fact that, at his age, he can come out physically and do the things he does every night, that's what really makes me marvel."

"I've been watching him for—what is it? 12, 13 years?—and he showed me moves I've never seen before," Jerry Reinsdorf said. "Bill Russell once asked me what was the greatest thing about Michael, and I said it was his determination. Russell said, no, it was his imagination. He certainly had imagination tonight."

Reinsdorf was asked if Jordan's big night was a perfect dividend on the $30 million, one-year contract the team had given him. "He's earned it," the chairman said. "I've never had any regrets."

OH ATLANTA

The Atlanta Hawks stepped up as the Bulls' next hurdle in the Eastern Conference playoffs and promptly claimed Game 2 of the series. For the first time in their incredible two-year run, the Bulls had surrendered home court advantage in the playoffs. In fact, Atlanta became the first visiting team in two years to win a playoff game at the United Center. Chicago had won 39 games against only two regular-season losses on their home floor over each of the past two years. During that same period, the Bulls had been 13-0 in home playoff games.

Now, however, the Bulls were facing back-to-back weekend games in Atlanta, leaving Pippen to warn that "unless we do the things we did all season to get 69 wins, we're not going to pull another win out of this series."

The Bulls seemed far from the togetherness that Jackson was urging. Pippen, in particular, seemed perturbed with Rodman who had struggled throughout the postseason with his return from the knee injury and with the officials, who had greeted him every playoff game with a technical or two.

"We've got to have a big effort from Dennis," Pippen said in his postgame press conference. "If he's not going to lead us in rebounding, don't lead us in technical fouls, because we don't need those."

Jackson later addressed the comments in a team meeting, reminding his players to stick together. "It's very unusual for this team," Tex Winter said of Pippen's open criticism of Rodman. "Generally they've been very supportive of each other... Phil handles this by saying simply, 'We're not pointing fingers at each other. Let's go out and do our jobs.'"

The other concern for the coaches was that Jordan, who had hit just 12 of 29 from the floor in Game 2, suddenly seemed to be pressing on offense, as if he felt he had to carry the entire load. "If he's not shooting any better percentage shots than that, then he shouldn't be taking so many of them," Winter said. "Phil's told him not to force things, not to try to do too much. To move the ball. And Michael knows that. Michael's a smart player. But he's so competitive and he's got so much confidence in himself, that it's hard for him to restrain. I've never been associated with a player—I don't think anybody has— who has any less inhibitions than he does."

It was pointed out that Winter was taking the diplomatic way of saying Michael had no conscience. "Well, that's one of the reasons he's a great player," Winter replied. "He has no conscience."

Yet Jordan clearly had a sense of team. With little or no complaint, he complied with Jackson's request to ease up on his aggressiveness. Although Rodman's situation saw no improvement, the Bulls rediscovered their team concept and took two games from the Hawks in Atlanta.

Then the Bulls closed out the series back in Chicago, where Rodman scored seven quick points to stake the Bulls to a 33-27 lead and went on to finish the contest with 12 points (including a pair of three-pointers), nine rebounds, three assists and a steal. He even blocked one of Dikembe Mutombo's shots.

The Worm was ejected after a profanity-laced exchange with the Atlanta center in the fourth period, but by then he had provided the hypercharge his team needed to subdue the

Hawks, 107-92, and claim the series 4-1. It was a grand way to celebrate his 36th birthday, and the crowd soon awakened to the presence of the old Dennis.

RILEY TIME

The victory sent the Bulls to their seventh appearance in the Eastern Conference finals in nine seasons, this time to face Pat Riley's surprising Miami Heat club. There was little doubt that meeting Riley still struck a match to Phil Jackson's competitive fires. An upset loss to Riley's Heat late in the 1996 season had prompted Jackson to enter the locker room and tell his players, "Never lose to that guy."

So the 1997 Eastern Conference finals became a showdown of coaching styles, Jackson's cerebral approach versus Riley's intensity. Chicago's triangle offense up against Miami's clutching, snakebiting, overplaying defense.

The Heat had won 61 games, mainly because point guard Tim Hardaway, in his second season playing for Riley, had gotten comfortable in his surroundings and turned in an All-Star year. In Game 1, though, Rodman's rebounding and the Bulls' pressure defense propelled Chicago to a win.

"The thing that shocked me the most is just the way we got taken apart at the end," veteran Heat reserve Eddie Pinckney said after watching his team lose the first game. "The Bulls are able to pressure on all the trigger points of your offense. Next thing you know the shot clock is down and you're throwin' up a shot from 30 feet out, or you commit a charge or something. It's like a blitz defense."

Pinckney remarked that that air of confidence was tangible in the United Center, and it wasn't something that other teams liked. "I guess it's routine for teams to come in here and play hard and still lose at the end," he said. "The Bulls are entitled to that attitude."

Actually, neither team had managed to shoot the ball well in the atmosphere of frenzied defense, set in motion by Riley's brand of scrambling, holding, bumping, brushing or anything else that worked. The final for Game 2, a 75-68 Bulls' win, set an all-time NBA playoff record low for scoring. Not since the days before the 24-second shotclock was installed had teams turned in such meager totals.

Hardaway, Miami's main weapon, was just five for 16 from the field. And Jordan made only four of 15 attempts. "Both teams were frustrated with their offensive play," Jackson said.

"We played ugly against Atlanta. We played ugly against Washington. It isn't the competition. It's just us. Except for our defense. Our defense has won games," Jordan, whose 23 points included 15 free throws, told reporters afterward. "Our offense has kept people in the stands. Defense has been winning championships for us in the past."

Behind the scenes, the Bulls' coaching staff spent hours reviewing the tapes of the first two games and came up with a plan to spread their triangle offense, an adjustment they had rarely used over the years. To say the least, it caught Riley and his players flat-footed and opened the back-door lanes to the basket for an array of layups and slams in Game 3. The Bulls exploded with a 13-4 run to open the second quarter and another 11-0 streak midway through the third.

The Miami crowd sat miserably, with only Rodman's new dye job—he shifted from his fundamental blond to another wacked out multihued look—and dark purple fingernails to keep them entertained as the Bulls smoked their way to the finish, 98-74.

"We got embarrassed out there today collectively," Mourning admitted afterward. "They just did what they wanted to do out there, and we did nothing to counter it.

"It's tough to stop a team like that because they've perfected their offense so well. If one part of their offense breaks down, they're able to go to another option."

It was as well as the triangle offense had ever functioned against an aggressive defense, Winter said, adding quickly that the Bulls' previous championship teams, featuring John Paxson and Bill Cartwright, probably executed the offense better than the current group.

The other part of the Chicago equation was the Bulls' trusty defense, which included a fine low-post effort from Rodman. Chicago had forced Miami into 32 turnovers. "It's almost like an amoeba defense," Riley said. "They take away angles. They deny your trigger passes. They're long. They switch on everything. They are an exceptional defensive team. You can't rely on just scoring in your half-court. If you're not running and rebounding and getting second shots at every opportunity you get, then it's gonna be very difficult to score."

MICHAEL GOES GOLFING

It seemed foolhardy at the time, but who could have known that Jordan would decide to play 45 holes of golf on his day off between games? Who would have figured His Airness to make just two of his first 22 shots in Game 4?

Yet no matter how deep a hole he dug for himself and his teammates, Jordan found a means to bring them rushing back at the end. Finding themselves down 21 points with the clock eating away the second half, the Bulls abandoned the triangle offense that had worked so well just the day before and watched Jordan go into his attack mode.

The Heat surged right back at the beginning of the fourth, pushing their margin back to a dozen, 72-60. Jordan then scored 18 straight points for Chicago, a display that trimmed the Miami lead to just one with only 2:19 to go. The ending, however, came down to the Heat making a final six free throws, good enough for a Miami win.

Jordan had scored 20 of Chicago's 23 points in the fourth quarter. "When he started making them, they just came, came, came, came, came," said Tim Hardaway. "He's a scorer, he's the man."

The good news in Game 4 was another outstanding effort from Rodman, who finished with 13 points and 11 rebounds, a performance he would nearly equal back in Chicago in Game 5 with another 13 rebounds and nine more points.

Jordan, too, continued on his tare from the end of Game 4.

He opened Game 5 with 15 in the first quarter, good enough for a 33-19 Bulls lead and little doubt as to the outcome. The only cloud as they closed out the Heat, 100-87, was a first-quarter foot injury to Pippen that kept him on the bench the last three quarters.

"They are the greatest team since the Celtics won 11 in 13 years (from 1957-69)," Riley told reporters afterward. "I don't think anybody's going to win again until Michael retires."

SILVERADO

The Utah Jazz, winners of 64 games, emerged from the Western Conference playoffs to challenge the Bulls in the 1997 Finals.

To get his players ready for the championship round, Phil Jackson brought yet another movie out of the dustbin, "Silverado," a 1985 Western starring Kevin Kline, Kevin Costner and Danny Glover as good outlaws who take on the bad sheriff in a western town.

"It's one of those quick draw movies, quick gun movies," Tex Winter said, "and I guess the key to it is that you better react quicker than the opposition."

And certainly shoot better than they do.

That became imminently clear on Sunday, June 1 in Game 1 of the 1997 NBA Finals, broadcast to a worldwide audience. The comforting sight for Bulls fans was Pippen grinning broadly in pregame warmups. He hopped around on his feet and seemed very ready to go, despite having suffered a foot injury in Game 5 against Miami.

The other welcome sight for old-time Bulls fans was Utah coach Jerry Sloan, hands jammed in pockets, awaiting the introductions, scanning the Chicago crowd, better heeled and not as rabid as the one that used to cheer him on in old Chicago Stadium. For almost a decade, Sloan had been "Mr. Chicago Bull" during his playing days in the Windy City, leading the Bulls with his hard-nosed, physical style of play. He had even served as an assistant and later the team's head coach, right up until his firing in 1981.

Sloan had virtually cut his heart out to get to the Finals for eight seasons as a player in Chicago. In this most delicious of ironies, he had finally reached it, to face his old team, the team that had retired his number 4, now hanging as a banner at the far west end of the building, one of only two jerseys honored in the United Center rafters, the other being Bob Love's number 10. Sloan and Love had been teammates on Bulls teams that put together a run of 50-win seasons in the 1970s and came achingly close to playing their way into the 1975 championship series.

MVP!

Utah's Karl "The Mailman" Malone had been named the league's regular season Most Valuable Player with the announcing of the balloting just a few days earlier. He had narrowly edged Jordan, the prime contender and four-time winner of the award. Jordan said he didn't mind the Jazz power forward getting the individual honor so long as the Bulls claimed the team championship at the end of the playoffs. Now the stars and their respective teams were meeting to settle the matter on the court, with fans in both Chicago and Utah eager to seize on the issue, chanting MVP! when one or the other stepped to the free throw line at key moments throughout the series.

The Jazz rushed out to a solid start in Game 1 by throwing quick double-teams at Jordan and working the boards hard, good enough for a quick Utah lead.

The Bulls obviously felt the tension, evidenced by their 40 percent shooting in the first half. Utah was slightly better at 44 percent, with John Stockton scoring 11 and Malone 10. Utah's Bryon Russell hit a three-pointer just before the buzzer to give the Jazz a 42-38 halftime lead.

Jeff Hornacek scored 11 points in the third period to help keep Utah in the lead, except for a brief run by Chicago that netted a one-point edge. The fourth opened with Utah clutching a two-point lead in the face of a mountain of Chicago's trademark pressure.

With just under eight minutes to go, Stockton hit a jumper, pushing the Utah lead to 70-65, which Harper promptly answered with a trey. Surging on that momentum, the Bulls managed to stay close and even took a one-point edge on a Longley jumper with three minutes left.

Malone responded with two free throws, but Harper snuck inside for an offensive rebound moments later and passed out to Pippen for a trey that put Chicago up, 81-79. For most teams, that would have been enough pressure for a fold, but Stockton hit a three of his own with 55 seconds left to make it 82-81, Utah.

Then at the 35.8 mark, Hornacek fouled Jordan, who stepped to the line with the building chanting MVP. He hit the first free throw to tie it, then missed the second, sending the crowd back to its nervous silence. The Jazz promptly spread the floor and worked the shotclock. As it ran down, Stockton missed a trey, but Rodman fouled Malone on the rebound.

As Malone prepared to shoot his free throws, Pippen whispered in his ear, "The Mailman doesn't deliver on a Sunday." To ensure that, the crowd raised a ruckus. His first shot rolled off the rim, and the building exploded in celebration. He stepped back from the line in disgust, then stepped back up, wiped his hand on his shirt, dropped eight short dribbles and missed again, bringing yet another outburst of delight from the crowd as the Bulls controlled the rebound with 7.5 seconds left. "I'm from Summerfield, Louisiana, and we don't have any excuses down there. So I'm not going to use any," Malone would say later. "It was agonizing, but I won't dwell on it."

Amazingly, the Jazz decided not to double-team Jordan on the last possession. Pippen inbounded the ball to Kukoc, who quickly dumped it off to Jordan, who executed a move on Bryon Russell and broke free just inside the three-point line on the left side. The entire building froze there for an instant upon the release of the shot. When it swished, 21,000 fans leaped instantly in exhultation. The shot gave the Bulls the win, 84-82, and the Jazz sank instantly, knowing they had just lost any hopes they had of controlling the series.

Asked afterward who deserved the MVP, Malone replied, "Obviously, it's Michael Jordan, no matter what Karl Malone says or not. Michael wanted the ball at the end and made the shot, and it's hard to argue with that."

Jordan had finished with 31 points on 13-of-27 shooting, while Malone rebounded after missing seven of his first eight shots to score 23 on the night with 15 rebounds.

"I think anyone watching anywhere in the world knew who would take the shot," Stockton said of the game winner.

"We ran the play to perfection," observed Pippen, who finished with 27 despite his sore foot. "We gave Michael the ball and told him don't leave them any time on the clock. He just eyed it out and took the shot he felt good about."

"The double-team never came and I knew I was in a one-on-one situation," Jordan said. "I crossed over, he went for the steal, and I moved to my left and put up the jump shot."

The Bulls opened Game 2 three nights later as loose as the Jazz were tight, and the scoring showed it. Jordan hit a jumper, then Pippen finished off a Harper back-door pass with a sweet little reverse, and moments later Longley broke free for an enthusiastic stuff. Like that, the Jazz were in a maze and couldn't find their way out.

Long known for their sadism, the Bulls' game management people had set up Part II of Malone's little chamber of personal horrors by declaring it clacker night and passing out noisemakers by the thousands to fans as they entered the building. A similar ploy had completely unnerved Miami's Alonzo Mourning in the first round of the '96 playoffs. Now it was The Mailman's turn.

When Longley fouled Malone 90 seconds into the game, the clackers were waiting and rattled him into two free throw misses. Two minutes later, when Malone went to the line again with the Jazz trailing 8-1, the whole barn was rattling like a giant playpen. This time, Malone stepped up and hit both. Given a momentary rush of confidence, Utah closed to 14-13 at the 4:41 mark of the first period.

Jordan was afire, though, and quickly squashed any momentum with a trey and a jumper. Then he fed Kerr for a pair of treys, and like that, Chicago had stretched the lead to 25-15 with 1:30 left in the period, which had 21,000 fans on their feet clapping and pounding to "Wooly Bully."

The Jazz dug in and made a run in the second period, bringing it to 31-29 with a Malone bucket. Just when it seemed Utah might find some life, the killer emerged in Jordan. He drove the Bulls on a tare to a 47-31 lead, scoring and drawing fouls like only he could. At every trip to the free throw line, the fans greeted Jordan with lusty chants of MVP! MVP!

When Kukoc hit a trey midway through the third period, Chicago had forged ahead 60-40. Yet Jordan was far from through. He took a feed from Kukoc on the high right post, quickly circled the defense hard right along the baseline, intent like some shark moving in for the kill, then knifed in at the appropriate moment to cut through an opening for one of his eye-popping reverses, one of those Jordan gymnastic feats with a 9.5 degree of difficulty. Before the fans had even settled back into their seats from cheering, he followed it up with a deep two that pushed the lead to 70-48.

How big was his hunger? That seemed to be the only question. Jordan finished the night with 38 points, 13 rebounds and nine assists. He would have registered a triple-double if Pippen hadn't blown a late layup, costing him the 10th assist. No matter, the Bulls coasted to a 2-0 series lead, 97-85.

"I thought we were intimidated right from the beginning of the game," Sloan said afterward. "If you allow them to destroy your will to win, it's hard to compete."

HIGH TIMES

The series then shifted to Utah, where the 4,000-foot altitude in Salt Lake City had the Bulls winded for the better part of a week. The team stayed in the nearby ski resort of Park City, which had an elevation of about 8,000, in hopes it would help the players adjust. But the Jazz took a 61-46 halftime lead in Game 3 and did a little coasting of their own, pulling the series to 2-1 with a 104-93 victory, during which Jazz fans showered Malone with their own MVP chants. He answered their support by scoring 37 points with 10 rebounds to lead the rout.

Game 4 on Sunday, June 8 unfolded as what was easily the Bulls' biggest disappointment of the season. Their offense still sputtered, but their defense for 45 minutes was spectacular. In short, they played well enough to win and should have. With 2:38 to go in the game, they had willed their way to a 71-66 lead and seemed set to control the series 3-1.

But Stockton immediately reversed the momentum with a 25-foot three-pointer. Jordan came right back with a 16-foot trey, and when Hornacek missed a runner, the Bulls had a chance to close it out. Instead, Stockton timed a steal from Jordan at the top of the key and drove the length of the court. Jordan recovered, raced downcourt and managed to block the shot, only to get whistled for a body foul, a call that might not have been made in Chicago, Jordan later pointed out.

Stockton made one of two free throws to pull Utah within three. Pippen then missed a corner jumper, Stockton was fouled and made both with 1:03 left to cut the lead back to 73-72. Jordan missed a jumper on the next possession, Stockton rebounded and looped a perfect baseball pass down to Malone for a 74-73 Utah lead.

The Bulls' next possession brought Kerr a wide-open three-pointer from the right corner that missed. With 17 seconds left, Chicago fouled Malone, setting up repeat circumstances from Game 1. Would he miss again in the clutch? Pippen wanted to talk to him about that, but Hornacek stepped in to keep him away from the Mailman.

"I knew what he was doing, trying to talk to me," Malone said. "He still talked to me the whole time I was shooting."

Pippen went into rebounding position and yelled "Karl!, Karl!"

His first shot knocked around the rim before falling in, smoothing the way for the second and a 76-73 lead. With no timeouts, the Bulls were left with only a rushed three-point miss by Jordan, which Utah punctuated with a breakaway slam for the 78-73 final, the second-lowest scoring game in league championship history.

"I guess The Mailman delivers on Sundays out here," Pippen acknowledged afterward.

Jordan had scored 22 points, and a foreign journalist asked him if he felt mortal. "There's gonna be games where I can't live up to the fantasy or the hype of what people have built up Michael Jordan to be," he replied. "I'm accustomed to living with that."

After moving at a breakneck pace, playing every other day, the NBA Finals slowed down again, giving the Bulls an agonizing three-day wait before pivotal Game 5 on Wednesday. Asked about the time off, an obviously despondent Steve Kerr said, "I try not to think about it. It hasn't been fun."

Actually none of the Bulls seemed too relaxed. Kukoc was shooting 34 percent for the series and averaging 7.5 points. Kerr had made only three of his 12 trey attempts. Harper was shooting 33 percent and averaging 5.5 points. Rodman was averaging a little over five rebounds in each of the first four games. Even Jordan, who had shot 51 percent in the first two games, had seen his shooting drop to 40 percent in the next two.

"They're giving us everything we can ask for," Pippen said of the Jazz. "Five, six days ago, everyone was predicting that we would sweep this team. Now everything is turned around."

Just when it seemed the Bulls' predicament couldn't get worse, Jordan came down with a viral illness in the wee hours before Game 5. The first shock of the news hit his teammates at the morning pregame shootaround. He was too sick to attend. Jordan miss a practice? Never.

"It's kinda scary," second-year forward Jason Caffey said, sitting wide-eyed in the locker room before the game. "You don't know what's going on when it's like this."

Never had a Bulls locker room been so quiet. About the only sound in the room was equipment man John Ligmanowski whistling as he worked, trying to cut the tension. In the darkness of the training room a few feet away, Jordan lay like some sick puppy. However, some veteran Bulls observers weren't fooled. "Michael's sick?" one asked. "He'll score 40."

Actually the total came to 38, including the back-breaking three down the stretch to deliver the Bulls from the dizzying altitude. Despite his well-known flair for the dramatic, this performance was no act. "I've played a lot of seasons with Michael and I've never seen him so sick," Pippen said afterward.

The Jazz came out strong, riding on the emotion of their crowd and the confidence of their 23-game home winning streak. Jordan scored Chicago's first four points, then faltered weakly while Utah rushed out to a 16-point lead early in the second quarter, 34-18, on an Antoine Carr jumper.

Jordan, though, fixed his focus on the rim and started taking the ball inside. He contributed six points on a 19-6 Chicago run that pulled the Bulls to 42-39. Malone, meanwhile, was forced to sit with an early third foul. Jordan's inside work also produced eight free throws in the quarter and helped give Chicago its first lead, 45-44. Malone again found more foul trouble in the third as the pace slowed, but Utah forged a five-point lead to start the fourth and expanded it to eight early in the quarter.

Then came Michael Time. He scored 15 points down the stretch to shove the pressure right at the Jazz. The Bulls were down by one when he went to the free throw line with 46 seconds to go. He hit the first, but snatched up the loose ball when he missed the second. Moments later he hit a three on a pass from Pippen, pushing the Bulls to an 88-85 lead.

Utah's Greg Ostertag scored on a dunk to cut Chicago's lead to 88-87 with 15 seconds left, but on the ensuing inbounds play Pippen dribbled into the open court and found Longley underneath for a slam. Up 90-87, the Bulls relied on their defense to force Hornacek into an off-balance three-pointer. The Jazz controlled the miss, and Stockton made a final free throw. But the Bulls had ridden their championship experience to a decisive 3-2 series lead. Jordan stood under the Utah basket jutting his fists into the air triumphantly as the game ended.

"I almost played myself into passing out," Jordan said. "I came in and I was dehydrated, and it was all to win a basketball game. I gave a lot of effort, and I'm just glad we won because it would have been devastating if we had lost..."

He had hit 13-for-27 from the field with seven rebounds, five assists, three steals and a block.

"He hadn't gotten out of bed all day, standing up was literally a nauseating experience, and he had dizzy spells and so forth," Jackson said. "We were worried about his amount of minutes, but he said 'Let me play,' and he played 44 minutes. That's an amazing effort in itself."

The Bulls celebrate title number five.

FIVE ALIVE

The series finally returned to Chicago, and on the morning of Game 6 the players begged Phil Jackson not to make them watch more basketball video clips. "Let's just watch the end of Silverado," they said.

In the film, the group of good guys had become fragmented only to come together at the end for a glorious shootout with the bad guys. Sensing the mood had built just right, Jackson agreed to run the tape through to the end.

Togetherness, of course, was the clear and perfect answer to the predicament.

Jordan finished the season's business that night. A perfect

Hollywood kind of ending. The Jazz valiantly took the lead early and kept it until the Bulls' pressure finally ate it away down the stretch, with Jordan driving the issue. Thirty-nine more points and two hours of defense, all capped off with the sweetest little assist to Steve Kerr, the same Steve Kerr who had been groaning in his sleep and talking to himself because he had missed a wide-open three that could have won Game 4.

"Steve's been fighting with himself because of Game 4," Michael explained afterward. "He missed a three-pointer, and he went back to his room. He doesn't know this. His wife told me he was very frustrated. He kept his head in the pillow for hours because he let the team down, because everyone knows he's probably one of the best shooters in the game and he had the opportunity to pick us up and give us a lift, and he was very disappointed."

Always looking to use everything, Jordan knew that the desire for absolution would run strong at the end of Game 6. "When Phil drew up the play at the end, which everybody in the gym, everybody on TV knew it was coming to me, I looked at Steve and said, 'This is your chance, because I know (Utah's John) Stockton is going to come over and help. And I'm going to come to you. And he said, 'Give me the ball.'"

The response struck Jordan as something that John Paxson would have said. And all Bulls fans know how much Jordan respected Paxson and his ability to knock down that open shot, just as they know how Jordan and Kerr clashed after Michael returned to the team in 1995.

"Tonight Steve Kerr earned his wings from my perspective," Jordan said, "because I had faith in him and I passed him the ball and he knocked down the shot. I'm glad he redeemed himself, because if he'd have missed that shot, I don't think he could have slept all summer long. I'm very happy for Steve Kerr."

It was a brilliant, sweet, delicious cameo, one that Chicago will treasure. But the greater glory remained Jordan's because NBA championships ultimately are always a test of will, and for the 1997 title he produced the ultimate display of it, in sickness and in health.

"It's been a fight," he admitted afterward. "It's all guts, deep down determination, what your motives are, what your ambitions were from the beginning. There's been a lot of soul-searching. It's easy to sit back and say, 'I've given my best, I'm tired. Somebody else has got to do it.' Or whatever. I didn't take that approach. I thought positive and did whatever I could do. Every little inch of energy that I have I'm going to provide for this team."

He knew his teammates were following his lead. "If you give up, then they give up," he said. "I didn't want to give up, no matter how sick I was, or how tired I was, how low on energy I was. I felt the obligation to my team, to the city of Chicago, to go out and give that extra effort so that we could be here for the fifth championship."

Jordan and the Bulls had begun with a faithful coterie of about 6,000 in 1984. Along the way, they had added millions of fans, all captivated by his Air Show. In 1891, Dr. James Naismith had set the height of the goal at 10 feet. More than a century later, it remained the same challenge. Yet there was little doubt in anyone's mind that Michael Jordan and his Bulls had elevated the possibilities.